The Essentials of Parental Alienation Syndrome (PAS)

It's Real, It's Here and It Hurts

By

Robert A. Evans, Ph.D.
&
J. Michael Bone, Ph.D.

The Essentials of PAS: It's Real, It's Here and It Hurts

Note to Readers: This publication is not intended to replace the advice and counsel of an attorney at law, nor the advice and treatment of a licensed mental health professional, but rather should be used in conjunction with professional services. The authors and The Center For Human Potential Of America, Inc. expressly disclaim any responsibility for legal consequences, loss or personal illness alleged to have been caused, directly or indirectly, by the contents of this book. If expert legal or mental health assistance is needed, the services of a competent professional should be sought. Throughout this book the readers are provided with recommended actions and suggestions, however, it is extremely critical that parents discuss with their attorney and or mental health professional before they act on any of the suggestions provided herein. There just may a unique circumstance in a case where this advice may be inappropriate. The situation should be thoroughly discussed and reviewed, all options should be gone over and consequences of one's actions need to be discussed before one acts. The professional experiences shared in this work are composites of actual cases. Special care has been taken to alter specific identifying features to protect confidentiality. Any resemblance to persons, living or dead is purely coincidental and unintentional.

The Center For Human Potential Of America, Inc.
2706 Alternate 19 North
Suite 214
Palm Harbor, FL 34683

Library of Congress Catalog Card Number: pending
ISBN: pending

Discounts on bulk quantities of this book are available to corporations, professional associations, schools, churches and other organizations. For details and discount information, contact the Special Sales Department at The Center for Human Potential Of America, Inc., Publishers: PHONE (727) 786-0600   FAX (727) 787-8193
E-mail: info@drbobevans.com.   Visit   our   websites: www.drbobevans.com and www.jmichaelbone.com

About the Authors

Dr. Evans has a Ph.D. from The Catholic University of America. He has over twenty-five years of experience in individual, group & family counseling; psychological & educational evaluations; training & training research. He is an approved sponsor of continuing education for psychologists by the American Psychological Association. In addition, he has been approved by numerous state bar associations to offer continuing legal education to attorneys in the areas of Parental Alienation, Parent Alienation Syndrome and Critiquing & Reviewing Child Custody Evaluations. He specializes in comprehensive divorce services, including child custody evaluations, expert testimony, attorney consultations and trial preparation. Dr. Evans can be reached at his website www.drbobevans.com or his email: drevans@drbobevans.com.

J. Michael Bone, Ph.D., holds a Ph.D. from the New School for Social Research in NY. He has worked extensively in the area of high conflict divorce with special interest in Parental Alienation. He has served as evaluator, therapist, court appointed expert, researcher, teacher and consultant. He currently serves in a consultative capacity to attorneys and

parents throughout the United States, and advises them on developing strategies and outcomes that protect their children's wellbeing, and their relationship with them. He has numerous publications and presentations on the topic of Parental Alienation Syndrome. Dr. Bone may be reached through his website, www.jmichaelbone.com or his email: Michael@jmichalebone.com.

Dedication

This book is dedicated to Richard Gardner for his intellect, courage and insight. Without his work as a basis, we would not have made the progress we have to educate - even more fully - both professionals and parents to change what can have a devastating effect on children and their families.

We would also like to thank our loving wives for their encouragement and patience walking with us on this path. We are thankful for their thoughtful contributions to our attempts in creating this book and helping us to make the material clear. And a thank you to all of our professional colleagues in the legal and mental health professions who continue to recognize and encourage our efforts.

Finally, we would like to thank all of the parents, whose involvement with parental alienation, taught us the tragic and hopeful lessons of their experiences in the hopes that we make them useful to others and protect both the children and their families in the future.

Bob and Mike

Preface

This work was compiled from a number of recordings of continuing legal education workshops and seminars that the authors had conducted over the last few years. In addition, the content was embellished with content from a number of papers that the authors published along the way. Some of these can be seen on the authors' websites, www.drbobevans.com and www.jmichaelbone.com . Also, the works of Richard Gardner (1998), the original author of the disorder referred to as Parental Alienation Syndrome, were reviewed and selected ideas and content are inserted into this work. Both authors are contributors to the proposed diagnosis for inclusion into the next edition of the Diagnostic and Statistical Manual published by the American Psychiatric Association and some of that work is include herein.

The authors are very grateful for having the experience and honor of working with Dr. Gardner when he was alive. He was a man of unusual talent, a prolific writer and a pioneer in the field of forensic psychiatry. Unfortunately, much of his work is misquoted, exaggerated and at times misunderstood. This book is simply a snapshot or overview of Parental Alienation and Parental Alienation Syndrome and should be used as an outline in working with this disorder. Readers are encouraged to read Dr. Gardner's works and others thoroughly in order to have a working knowledge in order to treat children and families who have become victims of this terrible malady.

It is our sincere hope that professionals, including judges, attorneys, guardian ad litems, parenting coordinators, therapists, and custody evaluators, working with high conflict divorce cases where child custody is an issue consider the information presented and pursue further education about Parent Alienation and Parent Alienation Syndrome. It is said that there are three sides to a divorce case: his, hers and, just perhaps, this book tells the third side.

Foreword

This book, *The Essentials of Parental Alienation Syndrome*, is written by two well-known psychologists, Robert A. Evans and J. Michael Bone, and it is a tribute to the pioneer contributions of child psychiatrist Richard A. Gardner. Whenever there are new theories, concepts and practices that become well-accepted and established in a particular field, there are those professionals identified as the "old timers" and then there becomes a new generation of professionals that brings these concepts to a new level of understanding and practical implementation. Unfortunately, in the progression of developments in the field and the introduction of similar terminology to describe the fundamental phenomenon, the founders and the leaders often recede in the background. Instead of using the original term *parental alienation syndrome,* similar concepts have been introduced such as *parental alienation, divorce-related malicious mother syndrome, hostile parenting, brainwashing parent and divorce poison*. The latter term is well- recognized by the popular book for general public reading written by clinical and family psychologist Richard Warshak. The new wave is being led by forensic psychiatrist William Bernet who has led the informal task force of distinguished contributors to what now becomes a movement in support of the diagnosis of parental alienation and parental alienation syndrome to be included in the DSM-5 and the ICD II, see the textbook on this subject published in 2010. The term proposed for these diagnostic manuals is that of *parental alienation disorder.* There are over 600 professional references to PAS consisting of journal articles, books and papers presented at national conferences.

The last book written by Dr. Gardner was in conjunction with me and later joined by Demosthenes Lorandos, Ph.D., J.D. entitled *The International Handbook of Parental Alienation Syndrome: Conceptual, Clinical and Legal Considerations* which was published in 2006. The vision of Dr. Gardner was to provide an international perspective of appreciation that this form of emotional child abuse is not restricted to the United States or any particular ethnic or cultural group but rather is widespread throughout the world.

Recognition of the developments of Dr. Gardner's contribution began with his first book on this topic, *Family Evaluation in Child Custody Litigation* published in 1982, and it was followed by *The Parental Alienation Syndrome and the Differentiation Between Fabricated and Genuine Child Sex Abuse* in 1987. The unique contribution of this book, *Essentials of PAS* by Drs. Evans and Bone is the streamline compilation and synthesis based upon their analysis of the many diverse contributions of Dr. Gardner. Consider the prolific work of Dr. Gardner writings of about 40 books plus about 130 journal articles now being described in a pocket edition of 127 pages.

In this spirit, as editor of *The American Journal of Family Therapy*, last year introduced a change in the book review department. Included now are reviews "Oldies But Goodies" meaning that a book published 10 years ago should not be forgotten and we should be reminded of its seminal contribution as a classic textbook in the field. Selected for review in this category was Dr. Gardner's second edition of *The Parental Alienation Syndrome: A Guide for Mental Health and Legal Professionals* published in 1998. The first edition was published in 1992. This book by Evans and Bone is a welcomed and refreshing condensation that is now offered by the "old timers" who have known Dr. Gardner and lived during the times of the controversy in his contribution to the field.

During the developmental stages of the infusion of the contributions by Dr. Gardner, I, in particular, requested that he write the article *Misinformation Versus Facts About the Contributions of Richard A. Gardner, M.D.*, published in the *AJFT* in 2002. Dr. Gardner began the article quoting philosopher Arthur Schopenhauer as saying:

> *All trust passes through three stages:*
> *First, it is ridiculed.*
> *Secondly, it is violently opposed.*
> *Thirdly, it is accepted as self-evident.*

Parental alienation syndrome gained its well-known name during the mid-1980's but few professionals recognize that the history of this term preceded Dr. Gardner. What was missing, of course, was the benefit of his wisdom of conceptualization, diagnostic terminology and explanation of this phenomenon. Attorney Robert Franklin, in 2009, described the history of PAS dating back to pre-1985 PAS cases revealed in a varied terminology: "(an attempt to) alienate the affections of the child from the other parent" (Ball case, 1827); "poisoning the minds of the children against her" (Guillot case, 1877); "secreted the children for the purpose of alienating their affections from her" (Hyland case, 1883); "husband and his family have exercised an undue influence over the boy and has inoculated (him) with hatred toward her, so that he is now not desirous of seeing her" (Carter case, 1904). Albert Einstein is included in the list as an early father's rights campaigner when he divorced his wife Mileva Mari in 1919 and the theoretical physicist and Nobel prize winner lost meaningful contact with his three alienated children.

What is missing from many of the newer professional textbooks and popular public books for PAS victims on this topic is the basic and fundamental theory of causation, classification, and amelioration of what is happening. To the targeted parent is the identification that they are not alone and that many other parents who have become estranged from their children through no fault of their own as a result of an acrimonious divorce often with the personality of a borderline spouse displaying narcissism and possessing the qualities of being anti- social in the true sense of the word, an absence moral fiber and human consciousness of right and wrong in their malicious conduct to achieve their ultimate goal of a *parentectomy*. This book provides useful information and will be therapeutically helpful to its readers.

S. Richard Sauber, Ph.D., ABPP
Forensic family psychologist
Formerly, Professor of Psychology in the Medical Schools of Brown, Columbia and the University of Pennsylvania

Table of Contents

Parental Alienation Syndrome

Introduction

We are seeing an increase in high conflict, adversarial divorce cases in mental health practices and in the courtrooms around the country. These cases present with a significant amount of parental conflict and, as a consequence, represent a threat to the children caught in the middle of these conflicts. Curiously, there is a great commonality among these cases in terms of the tactics alienators use to separate a parent from his or her children. It is almost as if they, the favored parent, were reading from a published playbook. Many evaluators and clinicians include Parental Alienation (PA) as well as Parental Alienation Syndrome (PAS) in the same category when discussing this topic. PAS is acknowledged as being extremely controversial. It is controversial within the mental health profession and equally controversial within the legal profession. The purpose of this work is to share ideas, thoughts, background, theory and some experiences in working with high conflict families. It is important for professionals to get a sense of both sides of the PAS issue.

Whether one uses PAS as a term, the problems brought by these cases are very real. The reluctance to consider PAS by name in the psychological and legal communities tends to contribute to the perpetuation of the problem in a variety of ways. Like any other designation, PAS can be and is misapplied and misused. Whether or not it is the appropriate diagnosis or description of behavior in a case must be determined by facts of that case and supported by evidence and data from multiple sources. An appropriate diagnosis and identification of PAS, along with a description of the severity, can make the difference between timely and effective interventions or allowing parents and children to be scarred for the rest of their lives.

Chapter 1: Parental Alienation versus Parental Alienation Syndrome

First, Parental Alienation must be distinguished from Parental Alienation Syndrome. Parental Alienation (PA) refers to a child being alienated or estranged from a parent. There could be a variety of reasons for this break in relationship. The word "break" presumes a relationship existed at one time and then was severed. A possible reason for this break could be deliberate behaviors engaged in by one parent relative to the other parent that could be directed to or through the children designed to interfere with a parent's relationship with their child. There may be other reasons, however, that a child becomes alienated from a parent. Among these reasons are normal separation issues. Preschool children, for example, frequently display separation anxiety when leaving a bonded parent. Children's temperament and a parent's response to a separation issue can be key variables in how a child behaves; these have to be taken into account when considering alienation in a case. Also, one parent may be lacking appropriate parenting skills. Frequently a parent who has been on the periphery relative to child raising responsibilities, and with the onset of divorce or separation may be just beginning to assume a participatory role with that child, may experience some reluctance from the child to spend time with that parent. In addition, some children may display oppositional behavior as in going through a stage of rejecting one or both parents. In intact families this rejection may be developmentally normal. In divorcing families this rejection may require more immediate and intense therapeutic intervention.

So, while PA can involve one parent denigrating, criticizing and attacking the other parent in front of, and ultimately in conjunction with, the children it does not necessarily have to be the case.

Parent Alienation Syndrome (PAS), on the other hand, is considered a childhood disorder reflected in the behaviors that a child displays toward a rejected parent. PAS, however, is seen as a direct result of one parent's attempt, the primary source behind a child's rejecting behavior, to remove the other parent, commonly referred to as the target parent, from their children's lives. The alienating parent, frequently referred to as the favored parent, attempts to make it appear that it is the child who feels this way on their own, with the alienating parent claiming no part in the rejecting behavior. The medical term "syndrome" refers to a disorder as having a clearly identified source. In the case of Down's syndrome, for example, the identified source is a specific abnormal chromosome. In the case of PAS it is commonly the favored or alienating parent. Richard Gardner, MD, a psychiatrist, borrowed heavily from his medical background in making analogies between medical science and PAS.

A source of the controversy with PAS lies in the fact that we are dealing with human beings and all their imperfections. Targeted parents bring their own baggage to a relationship and ultimately to their divorce. As a consequence, they frequently make mistakes, become impatient with a slow moving legal system and their legal representation for not immediately "fixing" this obvious injustice. They become angry with spouses who are trying to exorcise them from their children's lives, and become frustrated with children who appear to be cooperating in a plot against them; and so, sometimes they do things that appear to support the allegations of the other parent. In other words, they make errors of judgment that reflect poorly upon them. Many in both the legal and mental health professions then point to these behaviors as validation that PAS does not exist and that it is a natural outpouring of a high conflict divorce. What gets lost or minimized in the discussion is the alienating parent's role in this process.

How PAS is accomplished ranges from the most subtle to the most obvious of strategies and beyond, with kidnapping being the ultimate and most dramatic tactic. But all tactics carry the common goal of attempting to eliminate a targeted parent from their child's life. PAS relies on the specific actions of an alienating parent. These behaviors are predictable and form an identifiable pattern. In an article published in the *Florida Bar Journal*, March 1999 by Dr. J. Michael Bone and Michael R. Walsh, the authors outlined four identifiable behaviors for PAS. The pattern of these behaviors forms four criteria for PAS which are:

1) Visitation or access blocking by one parent
2) False allegations of abuse or unfit parenting against a targeted parent
3) Deterioration in the relationship between a child and the targeted parent since marital separation
4) Exaggerated fear reaction on the part of the child at displeasing the alienating parent

When some or all four of these criteria are present, the stage is set for the development of PAS.

PAS Tactics
As noted above, a suspicion of PAS may evolve by identifying the presence of these criteria that commonly appear in a case. The criteria are listed and discussed below.

1. Visitation or access blocking by one parent
This refers to the phenomenon of one parent (alienating/favored) attempting, and at times succeeding, at preventing children from being with the other (target) parent. In the creation of PAS, one ingredient that is consistently present is the absence of the (soon to be alienated) child from the target parent's life. When a child is kept from seeing the target parent for an extended time, the potential for the child to become alienated is greatly enhanced. It is very difficult to successfully turn a child against a parent with whom they have or have once had a good relationship and the child continues to see that parent on a regular basis. The untruths and distortions told about the target parent are inconsistent with the child's experience; hence their truth. Therefore the child's positive ideas about that parent are continually

reinforced, strengthened and ultimately protected by the child's continued contact. Disruptions in visitation are a clear "breeding ground" for alienation. It is simply a necessary ingredient.

2. False allegations of abuse

In order to block visitation, the alienating parent, must provide reasons as to why the child should not see that other parent. Invariably, the reasons given are that the other parent is in some way abusive, neglectful and incompetent; therefore they pose a danger to the child. It is very important to realize at this point, that terrible lies are routinely told when this criterion is met. For the normal and reasonable person who does not routinely lie, the gravity of this is sometimes hard to grasp. Virtually everyone can understand and identify with exaggeration. This is a normal phenomenon that everyone does on occasion, under various circumstances. This is **not** what is being referred to here. What is being referred to here, although commonly begun as exaggerations, evolves into becoming a complete fabrication of reality regarding the other parent. What is vitally important to understand here is that this is a process engaged in routinely by an alienating parent. Interestingly, if this process continues long enough and intensely enough, the alienating parent actually begins to "believe" their lies and eventually, their story evolves into a complete delusion. This delusion or false belief once transmitted to the child is actually a Diagnostic and Statistical Manuel-Forth Edition (DSM-IV) diagnosis called Shared Delusion Disorder (DSM-IV: 297.3). That is, a common delusion shared by the parent and child. This was referred to by Dr. Gardner in the first edition of his book on PAS and in the second edition (1998) as an alternative diagnosis until PAS is officially recorded in the soon to be published DSM-V, if it is approved for inclusion.

The concept of "abuse" must be understood as existing on a continuum. The least overt false allegation of abuse might be seen as implying that the target parent's characteristics are different and are somehow inferior to the characteristics of the alienating or favored parent. This has been also referred to in the literature as allegations of "virtual abuse" which describes an overall sense that the target parent, who is frequently absent, is somehow inferior or impotent as a parent. On the other end of the continuum are the allegations that the target parent is overtly abusive, either physically or sexually. When these allegations are raised as a rationale to prevent visitation, this should be seen as a major motivation to carefully evaluate for the possibility of alienation.

The first and most important question is: "Is this parent really abusive or just incompetent?" All allegations of abuse must be taken seriously. If after evaluation the conclusions are that a parent was not abusive and his or her parenting is not incompetent, while the child or children are expressing abuse or incompetent sentiments, then another explanation for the children's allegations (denigrations) must be found. It is widely accepted and commonly known that truly abused children sometimes adopt a protective stance with their abusive parent. So an evaluator, Guardian ad Litem (GAL), therapist must look deeply into situations where the cry of abuse is heard, yet the child is withdrawing from the targeted parent's relationship. Of course, it is entirely possible that an abused or neglected child withdraws from such a parent, but those involved should probe deeply into the allegations, generate alternative hypotheses and develop as many collateral sources of information as possible in order to validate the child's claims. In conducting child custody evaluations or abuse investigations, the evaluator would be wise to derive explanations for the child's behavior other than PAS. That is, the evaluator would be wise to set out to *disprove* PAS and in the absence of being able to do so, then PAS should be considered seriously.

In addition, it is notable to hear a child say that they do not want to see their parent for reasons that are not in any way proportional to their degree of alienation. Examples of this include a child saying that they do not want to see their parent because they do not like their cooking, they make them eat broccoli, or that they take them to Disney World too much, or other such non-substantial reasons. These are actual claims made in cases.

This tactic of the alienating parent attempting to discredit the targeted parent, commonly referred to as "poisoning the well" with misinformation, is often revealed in school and medical documents. It is often found in these places because this is where data is collected from the parent with whom the child usually resides, often about the other parent. School records, for example, are notoriously out of date and incomplete. Alienating parents will freely and willingly provide the child's school with the temporary injunction for protection from physical harm as a means to "protect" the child and substantiate their case to the school staff. It is not unusual, however, for the temporary injunction to remain in the child's cumulative folder for years, long after the matter had been resolved. The alienating parent frequently disavows any involvement or knowledge in failing to remove an injunction or to update a child's school records. Schools are known for their attempt to stay distant with these conflicts, so until an official document specifically states the injunction is no longer in place, the old injunction remains in the child's file with the school unwittingly supporting the alienating parent which, by the way, actually lends support, in the child's mind, to the abusive and neglectful allegations levied against the target parent. Very common in these cases is a cycle of "validation" where the target parent is reported to "violate" the injunction or behave in a manner that lends credibility to the original allegations. The presence of an expired injunction in school records, a child participating in group counseling for abused children, a therapist championing an alienating parent's position are examples of, what could be referred to as "pseudo-validation" of the abusive nature of a target parent. Some therapists go so far as to write letters recommending supervised visitation, restricted contact by the target parent or some other "protective" measure for the child. Such actions, generally are highly unethical and commonly a violation of professional ethics and in some cases actually against state statues, as they are currently in Florida. Legal professionals, especially judges, make a note relative to these circumstantial pieces of evidence.

The significance of this sort of unsolicited documentation relates to its impact on the school. When it is successful, the school becomes drawn into the campaign of denigration. That is, it subtly but clearly conveys similar messages of denigration to the child. When this process is not successful, this is typically due to the tenacity of the targeted parent, who becomes assertive with the school, thereby establishing their own independent relationship with the school. Assertive target parents are relatively rare because all too often their behavior is interpreted as "aggressive" and potentially dangerous and is presented to the court as such.

3. Deterioration in the relationship between child and target parent

This criterion refers to the effects of the first two. That is, when children are isolated from what will ultimately become the alienated parent and when it is conveyed to them in subtle and blatant ways that the other parent is inferior, dangerous, incompetent and unloving; it is not surprising that the relationship with that parent deteriorates. This deterioration occurs on two levels: external and internal.

External deterioration refers to how a child behaves in the company of various audiences. For example, if very negative things are being said about one parent, but the child is not fully alienated from that parent, he or she will refrain from being affectionate with that parent when such affections might be observed or reported back to the alienating parent. The typical example of this would be the child who has little or no contact with the targeted parent at a sporting event while with the indoctrinating parent. This same child will then warm up to the same targeted parent when "no one is looking." These children are often described as being very "guarded." This sort of deterioration is very common in the early stages of most divorces, and is not necessarily representative of alienation by one parent. This avoidance by itself, therefore, should not be taken as being indicative of alienation by one parent against the other. When such alienation is present and this kind of external deterioration of the relationship with the other parent does not diminish with time, however, then deeper inquiry is warranted. When parental alienation is committed by one parent against another, the process of external deterioration will not decrease, but will increase.

Internal deterioration refers to the actual subjective deterioration of the child's view of the other parent. Under these circumstances, these children are often subtly rewarded for voicing criticism of the other parent, such as being given protective hugs and other affections in response to voicing them. When this occurs in the context of a parent who has been largely absent from the child's life, this internal process is accelerated, since there is less subjective data to counter the criticisms.

What is obvious here is that the child who is subjected to this process is presented with two competing views of the targeted parent. On the one hand, the child's own experience with that parent, being largely positive and without significant problems, portrays that parent in a positive light. This model is fed by the child's continued and ongoing contact with that parent and is therefore rich with detail and experience. For evaluative purposes, evidence that this view of the targeted parent is not present can be found in concrete and detailed experiences that occurred between that parent and the child. Therefore, to determine if internal deterioration is not present, one must probe the child and drill down for specific details and not settle for superficial generalities of their complaints regarding the targeted parent.

The other internal view or model of the parent in question is fed by the actions of the other parent rather than actual experiences between the targeted parent and the child. That is, this model may be formed by misinformation given to the child by the alienating parent. Such examples might be that

that the targeted parent did not want to have the child in the first place, or that they were abusive before the child could remember, or remind them of "abusive episodes" that had occurred when in fact their presentation consists of exaggerations of actual events and other such examples. Under these circumstances, when a child has been alienated by the actions or words of the alienating parent, details about specifics will not be forthcoming; there aren't any. Rather, criticisms voiced by the child about the targeted parent will be in very general terms and the child will not be able to elaborate on, or give context to what is being described. Frequently the same vocabulary used by the alienating parent will be presented by the child and at times claimed to be their own observations.

4. Fear reaction regarding displeasing the alienating parent

This criterion might best be summed up as "My way or the highway." In alienation cases, it is not uncommon for the alienating parent to respond to protests by the children by actually rejecting them. Since these children have been taught that they have already been abandoned by one parent, fear of further abandonment runs very deeply. It is important, therefore, to understand that the fear is actually a fear of loss of that remaining parent. It is this fear that fuels and drives the internal changes that occur in alienated children.

Closely associated to this is a behavioral pattern frequently seen in alienation cases that is an epiphenomenon of this fear. This related behavior is that of protectiveness. Often the alienated child, as a strategy to insure against further abandonment, becomes protective of the alienating parent. In these cases, the child will be told of the other parent's (the favored or alienating parent's) mistreatment and the child will come to the defense of the "wronged" (alienating) parent. This is very common. This pattern has the further complicating effect of generally placing the emotional wellbeing of the parent into the hands of the child. This is very burdensome to the child and ultimately very damaging. What is most important to understand, however, is that the core or underlying dynamic for all of these variations is fear of loss of the remaining or alienating parent.

While the first criterion is more easily identifiable in behavioral terms, this criterion is more psychodynamic by its nature and perhaps the most nuanced of the four criteria. It is the one that is most detected through clinical judgment and less through outward behavior. For example, this criterion might be considered present when the child is overtly fearful of the alienating parent, when they had just been rejected. This might also be detectable by observing the child as being agitated and generally angry with the alienating parent, perhaps after multiple rejections, coupled with positive incongruous experiences with the targeted parent. Additionally, this criterion might manifest itself as the child's expressing an inappropriate parental over-control with the alienating parent. For example, the favored parent is so over wrought with anxiety because the child is leaving for a weekend with the target parent that they cannot get out of bed. The child then assumes a parental role of "nursing" or caring for the favored parent. Also it is not uncommon to learn that the child sleeps with the favored parent out of concern for their wellbeing. In this formulation, the alienating parent is actually infantilized by the child. These are some of the myriad patterns that one can see between children and their divorcing parents that are often described as being "enmeshed." "Enmeshed" generally refers to blurred boundaries between children and parents, where lines of responsibility are misplaced, and blame is the theme of the day.

It might be said, that these dynamics and behaviors are commonly found in divorce, and post-divorce scenarios when parental alienation is not present. While this is quite correct, this criterion, however, may be determined as being present only when it includes all three other criteria. In other words, while these behaviors might be seen without Parental

Alienation present on occasion, when the other dynamics of alienation are evident, they serve to shape and intensify these behaviors very distinctly to a point where they become a relational theme. Put another way, when alienation is present this quality of enmeshment forms the core of the alienating/favored parent-child relationship.

While Dr. Gardner (1985 to 2006) has been the person most associated with PAS, there have been other professionals who have been involved in similar and related work but are rarely recognized. A similar happenstance in other sciences had also occurred. For example there is a remarkable similarity with work of such individuals as Charles Darwin and Alfred Russel Wallace. Although it is rarely spoken about, the theory of evolution was somewhat of an evolving event itself. The foundation for Darwin's theory was known for many years prior to his publication of the _Origin of Species_. Other scientists had evidence that life on Earth existed for a long time and that it changed over time with many species becoming extinct. Darwin was the first to show how all the prior evidence supported the evolution of species from a common ancestor. The prevailing thought of the day was that evolution was guided by a long-term trend of rising from a single-celled form to more complex ones. But it was Darwin and Wallace, working independently, who conceived a natural and observable way for life to change. Darwin called it _natural selection_.

Dr. Richard Gardner first referenced the term "parental alienation syndrome" in 1985 in his article _Recent Trends In Divorce and Custody Litigation_, published in _Academy Forum_. Gardner (1985) had an extensive background in working with children, especially in child custody and child abuse cases. He observed that the children he was evaluating would be extremely alienated from one parent and not the other. He would notice that it was unusual in the sense that normally, in most custody work, children tend to stay out of the middle and become an apologist for _both_ parents. Gardner's (1985) observations represented a significant departure from the norm; something else must be operating in these situations.

Gardner (1998) indicated that the concept of Parent Alienation Syndrome grew out of the adversarial environment of the courtroom. He reported that he observed children denigrating a parent while remaining very aligned with the other parent. He observed eight characteristics or symptoms that appeared in a consistent manner. These will be presented and discussed later.

Gardner's focus on PAS as a childhood disorder was unique, but beginning in the 1980's the professional literature has been presenting PAS-like descriptions in divorce cases including false allegations of abuse perpetrated to influence the custody decisions. At least three other "syndromes" have been identified. In 1986, Blush and Ross, unaware of Gardner's work, published the SAID syndrome, SAID stood for sex abuse allegations in divorce. Their work addressed cases involving falsely accusing parents, the child involved and the accused parent. Two other "syndromes" also found in the literature dealt with the rage and pathology of an alienating or falsely accusing parent. Jacobs in New York and Wallerstein in California published reports of what they called Medea Syndrome in 1988. Turkat described Divorce Related Malicious Mother Syndrome in 1994.

There is also a body of divorce related research which, without a name, that describes the PAS phenomenon. Clawar and Rivlin (1991), authors of *Children Held Hostage*, make reference to Gardner's PAS in their large scale study of parental programming in divorce and Johnston who wrote about high conflict divorce and the problem of children, who refuse visitation, included a discussion of PAS. Dr. Deirdre Rand (1997), in Part I of The Spectrum of Parental Alienation Syndrome stated:

> "when PAS is viewed from the standpoint of parts and subprocesses which create the whole, the literature which pertains increases

exponentially, for example: psychological characteristics of parents who falsely accuse in divorce/custody disputes; cults who help divorcing parents alienate their children from the other parent; and psychological abuse of children in severe PAS including Munchausen Syndrome by Proxy type abuse".

Interestingly in the decade prior to Gardner's discovery the legal and social environments were changing rapidly. The courts were changing from the "tender years" presumption to "child's best interests". In the "tender years" presumption, custody of children was almost automatically awarded to the mother. The presumption was that the mother was the primary care giver and therefore would be the "best" parent. The "best interests of the child" presumption focused on making custody decisions that would be intended to be in a child's best interest. Custody decisions, therefore, would not automatically be in the mother's favor, but depending on the circumstances of the case, fathers would be eligible as primary care givers as well.

Gardner (1998) and others noticed that with child custody decisions being based on circumstances rather than on gender of the parent, false allegations of child abuse began to rise. In fact, the increase was so dramatic that the National Center for Child Abuse and Neglect reported in 1988 that non-valid reports outnumbered cases of genuine abuse by a ratio of two to one (Clawar & Rivlin, 1991). It reached such a level that in 1993 the US Congress amended the Child Abuse Prevention and Treatment Act to eliminate blanket immunity for people who make false reports. They based their decision on data that showed 2,000,000 children were involved in false reports versus 1,000,000 genuine reports of abuse (Clawar & Rivlin, 1991).

While PAS is a psychological or psychiatric term, because PAS is founded in the legal arena, it is likely that this setting is the basis for the controversy surrounding it. The actual behavior patterns associated with PAS, that is, a child overtly behaves as if they do not want to be with the target parent, can be a means of convincing a court to award child custody to an alienating parent. In many cases courts will observe a child's alienation and assume there must be valid reason for the child's dislike of the other parent and err on the side of caution and restrict the targeted parent's access to the child. Frequently, judges, although contrary to judicial guidelines, will interview children alone and conclude that their case is simply a function of adolescent expressions of independence and dismiss alienation as a source of estrangement.

Many mental health practitioners will actually support an alienating parent unwittingly because they too do not want to subject a child to undo stress, so they will testify to a court that they support limiting a targeted parent's access. The movie, "Cramer verses Cramer", addresses this very subject and is an excellent example of a typical PAS situation.

Unfortunately, what is happening with greater frequency are false allegations of PAS. In this scenario the alienating parent not only alleges abuse by a target parent but levies allegations of PAS as well. The alienating parent produces "evidence" that the target parent is engaging in alienating tactics in order to sever their relationship with their child. The target parent is frequently fighting to reinstate visits, maintain visit or strengthen their relationships with their child. Their behavior is presented and interpreted as alienating tactics. A target parent, for example, may return a child late from a visit. Their tardiness will be exaggerated as an indication of their trying to alienate a child from them. This gets to be a very complicated situation to unwind.

PAS still continues to be controversial, although recently there is a dramatic increase in the level of acceptance and the diminishing of conflict between and among the legal profession and mental health practitioners. One, however, still comes across pleadings and articles that raise some of the same issues of criticism about PAS, which will be discussed later.

What Is Parent Alienation Syndrome (PAS)?

Technically, PAS is a childhood disorder where a child aligns themselves with one parent and is preoccupied with the denigration of the other parent. The vilification and denigration of the targeted parent is unjustified and exaggerated to the degree that the child's behavior is not warranted by the parent's actual behavior.

An important issue to understand is that PAS is more than brainwashing. A critical difference between PAS and brainwashing is that brainwashing refers to an echoing of what a child has been told by a coaching source. In the case of PAS the coaching source is an alienating parent and the child begins to make their own contributions to the campaign of denigration. They will begin to make things up. They will become the leading edge of the criticism of that one parent – what we refer to as the targeted parent. This is different from simply brainwashing, which is the result of deliberate active, as well as passive, coaching.

Basically what Gardner (1998) was arguing was that there was a combination of behaviors by the alienating parent designed to program the child. The child responded in like fashion and frequently imitated the alienating parent in this campaign against a targeted parent. It is this combination, the parent's behavior and the child's active involvement that is really the hallmark of PAS. It should be kept in mind that PAS is a subset or subcategory of alienation. Frequently, professionals will argue that there is no such thing as PAS in that it's all just alienation.

PAS is frequently being used rather loosely such as whenever a child appears alienated from a parent and that can be a great disservice and even an endangerment to the children. All alienation incidents are not necessarily one parent and child aligned against another at the hands of an alienating parent; there may be a number of reasons as to why a child may appear resistant to a parent.

Not All Parent Rejection Is PAS

While it may seem difficult to understand that any child could reject or even hate a biological parent in the absence of an apparently valid reason, when confronted with such a situation in a child custody case, one might jump to the conclusion that one parent is instigating that rejection. Courts, in these situations, are left with the difficult job of making sense out of these situations. Frequently, therefore, judges in custody cases need "experts" to tell them why a child is rejecting their parent.

There are a number of reasons a child can become alienated from a parent. The resolution to some of these cases may still be a court order for continued contact between parent and child so the problem can be resolved, either through natural interaction or with the help of therapy. If contact between a parent and child stops the relationship can morph into a phobic-like reaction to a parent who then becomes an alienated parent.

1. **Normal separation problems**. Preschool children usually go through some separation anxiety when leaving a parent. The extent that the anxiety is an issue is a function of the child's developmental stage, temperament and parents' response to the behavior. Visitation problems with a preschool child are similar to reactions to going to school for the first time and the situation requires similar techniques. The child needs to be reassured, lowering their anxiety while being steadfast that the transition will take place. Court orders enforcing the visitation time along with counseling and therapy focused on reassuring the "primary parent" and reducing their anxiety may go a long way to help. One can see that interrupting or terminating the visitation may only reinforce the anxiety and strengthen the "phobic-effect" to the targeted or alienated parent. Even in cases where PAS is demonstrated this recommendation is a preferred course of action.

2. **Skill Deficits in the non-custodial parent**. Quite often the non-residential parent is beginning to take responsibility and care for the children on their own for perhaps the first time in the child's life. Frequently, they do not have a complete understanding of the children's needs or have limited experience in parenting. Advice from one parent to the other is usually not received well, especially during litigation or just after the divorce. Generally, parent training will solve some of these problems. Sometimes, it is important to have the "novice" parent and children in counseling in order to help the parent understand the children's feelings and needs. Sometimes judges need to order a "novice" parent to buy things for the children so they'll have something to do or play with when they're visiting. It is surprising how literal one has to be with such parents.

3. **Oppositional behavior**. It is common for children to go through a stage of rejecting one or both parents, especially during adolescence and preadolescence. In intact families this rejection is not threatening and is developmentally normal. In a divorced or reconfigured family such rejecting behavior may require counseling in order to help set limits and negotiate a child's independence without ultimately sacrificing the relationship. The therapeutic assistance may become even more urgent as the reconfigured family matures and introduces step-parents and significant others into the equation. Here, "limit-setting" is essential while easing the child through the rejection stage.

4. **High-conflict divorced families**. In high-conflict divorces the children may need to escape the conflict by allying with one parent. Johnson and Campbell (1988), in their book, *Impasses of Divorce*, note that children around the age of nine usually ally with one parent in high conflict cases. This is a normal form of

adjustment. Unfortunately, on the surface there is an appearance of PAS but it may not be genuine PAS. Both legal and mental health interventions should focus on maintaining contact so the child can mature enough to stand outside of the conflict and form relationships with both parents. Counseling can help parents with what to do and what not to do in their interactions with the children. Probably the best therapeutic issue to focus on is to reduce the conflict between parents, sometimes easier said than done.

5. **Serious non-abuse problems**. There are situations in which there are serious problems in the relationship between the non-residential parent and the children, which are abusive, although do not always technically constitute reportable abuse. For example, parents who are alcoholic, extremely rigid and controlling, or have severe psychiatric disturbances may be rejected by the children. In such cases, the only way the children can tolerate being with that parent is in psychotherapy. In therapy a therapist is present who can "mediate" the impact of the parent's emotional problems on the children. However, it is still important that the child have some contact with the parent in order to form a realistic understanding of the parent and develop a workable relationship.

6. **Child abuse**. Physical and sexual child abuse occurs in divorced families just as it does in intact families. The therapeutic steps for such families involve protecting the child from the abusive parent until that parent takes responsibility, has been rehabilitated and has demonstrated change. These cases present the difficulty of knowing when visits can commence, when to begin monitoring visits, the length of visits, the duration of monitoring, etc. However, some form of contact between parent and child is still beneficial for the child after the parent shows readiness for appropriate interactions.

Clearly, given the above situations, not all alienation is PAS. Some alienation may also have a hint of legitimacy in the sense that that parent earned or deserved the child's rejection by their behavior as in being abusive, neglectful or absent. The key point, however, is to understand that there are ways to separate the two and to know which is PAS and which in fact is a legitimate consequence of abuse.

Definition of PAS
The official definition of PAS, therefore, is: PAS is a childhood disorder that arises almost exclusively in the context of child custody disputes. Its primary manifestation is the child's campaign of denigration against a parent; a campaign that has no justification. It results in the vilification of a targeted parent from the combination of tactics executed by a programming or alienating parent and the child's own contributions. So when there is true parental abuse or neglect, then the child's animosity may be justified, therefore, PAS may not be an appropriate diagnosis.

Like all rules there may be an exception. In other words, you might actually have an abusive parent, a child becoming alienated from a targeted parent and even though there is abuse present one may not rule out PAS. Sometimes in an abusive relationship the concept of "identification with the aggressor" is encountered. In such situations a child may identify with an abusive alienating parent. This identification process is frequently based on fear of the alienating parent. The child's rejecting behavior, therefore, is based on their fear of the alienating parent rather than on an acquired hatred of the targeted parent. The overt behavior may look the same with the child outwardly expressing hatred for the targeted parent, but is actually responding out of fear from the alienating parent. The child will maintain their position, hatred of the targeted parent, in a steadfast manner regardless of the therapeutic interventions.

This issue is one of the areas of controversy, where some theorists and some researchers in the field of divorce basically are saying something like: "this alienation by the child is a natural process and we see that in many of the high conflict cases and to call PAS as a special syndrome is incorrect".

Along these lines we've talked to a number of attorneys and their response is:

> "What's different about this from the other case that we have. They're all like this. You know we have one parent hating another parent, doing and saying things to children and sometimes we have children disliking a parent and so this is just sort of run-of-the-mill".

But in fact, there are differences and it is possible to determine the differences. It is very important for clinicians to know about this problem. Frequently when a child is alienated, oddly enough many clinicians, therapists and evaluators do not investigate the cause of the alienation, yet this is very important. This is astounding, yet a very common occurrence. It would be as if someone comes into a doctor's office and they have high blood pressure and unless the cause of that is determined, the doctor may treat it with the same medications as he or she treated someone else. But if the cause of the blood pressure is say active alcoholism that patient needs to be treated differently than if someone has high blood pressure due to stress.

Gardner found that this type of behavior is common in high conflict divorces. He argued that like medical science we need to look for finer and finer levels of information about particular disorders. To really support children and have them in the best environment and help parents we need to continue to examine in ever greater detail what is going on in our divorce cases.

So saying somebody has heart disease is not particularly helpful. But identifying a specific subcategory of heart disease starts to address the type of treatment and leads to the etiology of the disorder. He was really a proponent of applying the same medical model to discovering the nuances of PAS.

PAS is a specific disorder with the definition having to do with the actions of one parent; the improper actions of one parent in conjunction with the child for the purpose of turning that child against the other parent. Psychologically, it is turning a love object into an object of hate. It is also very important to state that because we are working with human beings, mistakes and errors in judgment will be made. While PAS is instigated by one parent, the target parent is frequently not without fault. What we find, however, is it these faults are exaggerated and used as a basis for the alienation process.

There may be a variety of motives behind the execution of PAS. It could be to change residential custody, or sole custody instead of shared or joint custody. A parent may want to get the other person out of their life. Revenge is another motivation. We haven't gotten there yet in terms of discussing motives behind PAS. We're just now talking about the actual disorder, defined by Richard Gardner along with some of the issues that are surrounding PAS.

When children are alienated by PAS, that is, by the actions of one parent to influence that child against the other parent, there is a certain theme that you see over and over again, and that is the child acts as though the target parent is a monster. They act as if that parent has done terrible things to them. They also act as though they have been severely abused by that parent. They will frequently make up things that never could have actually happened and yet they claim that they did. Often in the earlier stages of PAS, you will see children beginning to pull away from a parent and the reasons they are giving for doing so are completely inconsistent with the level of alienation. That is one of the hallmark signs and we'll get into more depth on this in a while.

Reasons It Appears To Be Increasing

One of the reasons that we are seeing an increase in PAS in the legal system and in the mental health practices is that we are noticing a new evolution of courts leaning very heavily in the direction of shared or joint custody. The word "custody" has been exorcised from court proceedings and substituted with timesharing and parenting plans. Equal timesharing has frequently been the default position of courts and one has to come up with reasons not to go into an equal time sharing arrangement. Frequently courts suggest it is in the child's best interest. So as a subset of the "best interests' issue, parents are fighting over children as if they are an object or prize in the adversarial case.

In the state of Florida the word "custody" has been abandoned because that denotes ownership. The statutory language now is "shared parenting" with a primary residential parent, most often being named. We are seeing more cases, however, where a primary residential parent is not named, so both parents are primary residential parents. There is generally a move toward increasing the secondary parent's access to the child much more than there was before. Judges will commonly make visitation every other weekend from pick-up Friday night through returning the child to school on Monday morning. Prior to this it typically was Friday evening until Sunday evening. We are seeing that expanding. We are seeing more and more judges also awarding rotating or roughly 50-50 visitations and there is a literature to suggest that is a very good thing.

Symptoms of PAS

The symptoms exhibited in a child's behaviors when they are in the process of being alienated from a target parent form a simple checklist.

The eight symptoms are:

1. Campaign of denigration
2. Weak frivolous or absurd rationalizations for the deprecation
3. Lack of ambivalence
4. Independent thinking phenomenon
5. Reflexive support for the alienating parent
6. Absence of guilt
7. Presence of borrowed scenarios
8. Spread of the animosity to the extended family of the alienated parent

Each of these will be covered in detail below. As with other syndromes not all symptoms are present in every case. The more that are present, however, the more clearly the syndrome exists. Also like other syndromes, the symptoms form a rather predictable pattern and the reader will see that these operate in a very predictable and impressive way.

Chapter 2: PAS Manifestations in Detail

Campaign of Denigration

In the campaign of denigration the child is typically obsessed with the hated parent. The word "hate" is an interesting concept because Gardner (1998) points out that the opposite of love is not hate. He says that the opposite of love is indifference. So, if you have a child that is expressing this quantity of hate, in the absence of justification (a key element for PAS), perhaps there is more love present than one would imagine. For example, if you don't have a good rationale for hating somebody and you seem to be preoccupied with an expressed hatred of that person, then the suggestion is perhaps there is more love, affection and attachment than what meets the eye.

It's important to think, for example, of children who have been abused or neglected by a parent going through a divorce; the children want to have nothing to do with that parent who has been abusive and neglectful. In an interview with them the typical presentation is that they do not lead the conversation with how much they hate that parent; it's just the opposite. The typical presentation by that child is to not even bring the parent up, or to dismiss them totally as being an insignificant issue; to act more indifferently, as Gardner (1998) suggested.

But what you see with children in PAS cases is that their focus is on the target parent. Their campaign of denigration reveals alleged abuses by a target parent and a refrain of how much that parent is hated. It is just the opposite of what is documented for actual abuse cases. Their presentation of complaints is similar to viewing an agenda that they are putting forward; informing an evaluator, in a very comprehensive manner, all of their abusive parent's faults.

So, in the conduct of a psychological or custody evaluation for a possible PAS case, for example, when a child comes in by themselves, they will commonly begin the conversation presenting terrible faults of one of their parents. Sometimes their presentation begins even before they are asked a single question, which should be somewhat of a clue to the evaluator. This approach is really fundamentally unnatural because in cases where there actually has been physical abuse and neglect the child typically doesn't start that way.

So the campaign of denigration is an expression of hate, dislike, not wanting to be near the target parent, describing them as never being a caring, loving parent and who never did anything with them as in a normal parent-child relationship. The target parent is described as being always absent from the child's life; they were simply never there.

Understand again, there is a combination of players. So conceptually, behind the child's denigration is an alienating parent who is providing all the descriptors and shallow details; feeding the "fire", if you will. The child is either catching up with the alienating parent and providing some of their own issues, or in many cases you'll find that the children are parroting much of what the alienating parent says.

A simple way to flush this out during the first session with the child alone is to ask the child, what did your parent, or whoever brought them in, say to you about coming here today? This is where we get a "machine gun-like, rapid fire" litany of complaints against the targeted parent. With younger children an evaluator will frequently get a response similar to this: "Well, my mom wanted me to make sure that I told you how bad my father was, and he did hit me a lot, and left me alone one night while he was out with his girlfriend and we didn't have anything to eat and I had to sleep on the floor."

Sometimes with children who are a little older and more sophisticated, will couch their complaints in their own words but will deny that anyone coached them at all. But they still present as if their mission is to convince the evaluator the target parent possesses many faults.

The campaign of denigration is like a public relations campaign to convince the audience, in this case an evaluator or therapist, about the abusiveness, neglectfulness and unloving of the other parent. Frequently the parent who brings the child will just sit back and shrug and go, "I wish they felt differently but that's just the way that they are". So the presentation carries the appearance that this is coming solely from the child and the connection for the relationship between the parent and child is sort of puppeteer, the puppeteer is often very successfully hidden.

The significant component is that the children are obsessed with their hatred. For example, when asked the question "what do you do with your mom or dad, what activities do you two do?" Typically they respond that they never do anything with the targeted parent. The parent doesn't have time for them. When was the last time they had a good time with them? Typically their response is "never or I don't remember". When asked to tell the evaluator specifically about the abuses they had experienced, there is not a lot of detail. They cannot go into any kind of depth or detail about the abusive situations.

Sometimes when there has been an injunction filed with an allegation of abuse and that child has had to repeat the story a number of times. The child may tend to deliver the "details" in a very rote, automatic, way, as if someone hit the play button to start a CD. In this case there will be details but they have been developed from telling the same story repeatedly and resulting from being asked many of the same questions over and over. One needs to listen carefully to recordings of these interviews or read the transcripts of the recording very carefully as the details will change.

The lack or absence of details can also come from the alienating parent's sharing some of the legal documentation with that child. So all the child gets to learn are some pat phrases that are listed on the legal documents, motions, orders, etc... about the other parent. These documents sound like statement of fact but frequently they are nothing more than allegations made by one party against the other. The difficulty with one parent sharing legal documents with their children is that the documents present allegations by one party against the other and is presented as if they are facts. Children typically cannot discern the difference, so it appears as if the other parent is in fact guilty of the allegations.

In the case of younger children when determining if a child has been coached one might hear words that are beyond their vocabulary. Generally speaking three-year olds do not commonly use the word "molested". And if asked directly what the word means, they will honestly tell the evaluator that they don't know! Be on the lookout for words not typically spoken by children of certain ages such as "inappropriate" or "abusive" or "molested". Young children typically do not use these words in their daily language. Certainly there are exceptions but listen carefully to a child's vocabulary and listen carefully to the vocabulary of the adults in the case. Frequently there are commonalities in vocabulary; as an evaluator you are looking for clues that certain thoughts did not emanate from that child.

It is important to keep in mind too that there's a reciprocal pathological relationship evolving. As the child is expressing their issues and complaints about a parent, the alienating parent is usually encouraging it. At a minimum, they're not discouraging it. They are not encouraging or fostering a loving, caring relationship with the other parent. In fact, at a minimum, their silence when the child goes in that direction is actually encouraging the alienating theme. If they break the silence they may encourage the child on by saying "and don't forget he did this or he did that".

Weak, Frivolous and Absurd Rationalizations for the Deprecation
The next symptom is the weak, frivolous and absurd rationalizations for this campaign of denigration. One of the most telling and clearest examples of this is the following

actual response from a ten year-old. When asked why don't you ever want to see your mom? The child said "Because she takes me to Disney World too much." He then went on to explain that she doesn't really want to be with him. She just wants to drop me off at Disney World although whenever this child had been to Disney World, it was at that child's request and the mother was with him the entire time. More common examples are: I don't like their cooking or their house is too clean or their house is too dirty – or all kinds of things that you might find children commonly complaining about. This includes things like calling a father a jerk or an idiot or other demeaning word and then when asked for an explanation as to why that person is a jerk or an idiot, etc... their answer is: "I don't know but he just is - he's just a jerk". One teenage girl talked about her father who happened to be from Alabama and had a very Southern accent. Interestingly, she had a Southern accent herself, but came up with hating him because of his accent. She said that was why she never wanted to see him again. When you really examine the responds you realize that they aren't rationale responses.

Lack of Ambivalence
The symptom of a lack of ambivalence is where there is absolutely no wavering. That is, a child is consistent in terms of having a commitment to their position or opinion about the targeted parent. That parent is an evil person, not any good and there is nothing good about that parent whatsoever and never was. When asked did you ever have a good time? Answer: Never.

Show them a picture of them together with that parent and they are smiling; appear to be having a good time at a birthday party or at a park. When asked what was going on in the picture and that they seemed happy; they can't explain their apparent joyfulness that is expressed on their faces. If probed further they will say something along the lines of: he/she (dad/mom) forced me to look that way or if I didn't, I would get punished so I had to. I had to pretend, or any number of illogical statements.

With this symptom, however, being one of the more significant or severe ones; when you see a child who presents with a lack of ambivalence that is an indication you might be dealing with a more severe degree of the disorder.

Independent Thinker Phenomenon
This is where the child professes that the negative feelings and thoughts you are hearing about the targeted parent are their own. Children will swear or be adamant that "no one told me to say this. Nobody put me up to this." Here is an opportunity to ask that first question: "What did your Mom or Dad tell you about coming here today". The response will be something along the lines of "I want to make sure that I tell you everything bad about mommy, all of the horrible things mommy did to me, or all the things that daddy did, etc." As an evaluator one needs to try and press for details, looking for in-depth explanations and details about the horrible things that the parent allegedly had done. Commonly in PAS cases there is no substance to the complaints. Frequently, they will terminate their tirade against a parent with something like: "and nobody told me to say this".

When a child makes such statements it is obviously an important point that they feel needs to be made. It carries the assumption that the evaluator must be thinking otherwise. So, their proclamation is just an attempt to remove any possibility that that might be the case. They thought of this either because they've been told or had been prepared in that way or because they know they haven't come up with it all in their own mind; it is manufactured or implanted.

Reflexive Support of the Alienating Parent
As you review the symptoms you will see how these start to link up, especially as these increase in frequency and duration; the alienated child demonstrates an unbridled support for the alienating parent. An alienating parent, assuming this is a deliberate and conscious process, would be very encouraging of the things that we are talking about. If the process is going on at an unconscious level, then they will

reinforce the occurrence unwittingly. They will not even be aware of it. But in the reflective support symptom, the child is suggesting, "as much as I hate the targeted parent, I am that much more positive and committed toward the alienating parent."

This symptom is elicited by asking questions if there is anything that they agree with or like about the targeted parent. Even in high conflict divorces where PAS is not present, children will in some ways endorse both parents' positions about different issues and if anything, there's an urgency to not take sides. Typically in the case of divorce, the children do not want to take sides and they do not like being put in that position. In PAS cases, however one sees children clearly taking a side and never taking a supportive position of the targeted parent. As with the other symptoms, this is fundamentally unnatural. These are things that just don't happen normally when people go through a divorce. The child has to be nudged significantly by one parent through some kind of indoctrination process.

Absence of Guilt
In severe cases there will be an absence of guilt frequently observed in the child. The absence of guilt has to do with the lack of caring or affection toward the target parent. There is an absence of any conscience about what is happening to their parent or their role in it. We have seen children sit in a room with the targeted parent and say terrible things directly to them. They say thing like "I hate you; I don't ever want to see you again." They will be asked, when the parent's not there, if you found out that your mom or dad has a terminal illness and was dying, would be dead tomorrow or very soon, how would you feel? When children have this degree of symptomatology, they will not be fazed by such questions; they will say "that would be the happiest day of my life". In short, they express that they never want to see that person ever again. They have no use for them, they've never been their life up to this point, there's no point in their being in there now, etc.

This is one of the more severe symptoms. We will typically not see this until PAS has been in the process for a while. This is a very chilling symptom because if one considers attachment theory, a child's sense of relationship emanates from their relationships with their parents. When you have a child who is this disconnected from one of their parents, they are going to have serious relationship problems later on in life. With the absence of guilt, it says a lot about their ability to empathize and function normally and truthfully in relationships. One conclusion that can be made is that when children do go through this process, at this level of dysfunction, it is tantamount to a crash course in how to develop a personality disorder. It creates an individual who will be manipulative as an adult, who will have difficulty empathizing, who will tend to not be able to see other people's perspectives or be honest in their communication. While the research is still going on in this area, the dysfunctional dynamics being taught to children strongly suggest that this may be a reasonable hypothesis.

When the PAS enters the context of the legal system an alienating parent may successfully convince a court that a targeted parent is a truly bad parent and horrible person. Given this description of the target parent, the court should minimize or eliminate the targeted parent's contact with their child. The child will observe that if those tactics are very effective. They will learn that this is how you get what you want in life. And depending on how thoroughly this is done and how long the process takes, the child could start believing, like their alienating parent, that the things that have been said about the targeted parent must be true. If the child is left untreated, it is not inconceivable that they will eventually morph into a psychotic disorder, a delusional system that is a shared fixed delusion.

Borrowed Scenarios
Frequently one will hear a child say about a target parent "my father didn't want me to be born; he wanted my mom to have

an abortion". Obviously, no child would know that unless they were told by someone; the most likely person to do that would be the other parent. An evaluator will hear words or phrases that are common to both a parent and a child. The terminology will be repeated with the alienating parent coming in during their interview. They will use some of the same vocabulary and the child will come in and the evaluator will get very similar phraseology, if not exact vocabulary. This echoing of the vocabulary is more than a coincidence.

Spread of Animosity to the Extended Family of the Alienated Parent

There is a spread of animosity to the extended family of the targeted parent and especially significant others that enter the relationship. When the targeted parent gets into another significant relationship with someone, very often this can initiate the PAS process.

Even after the marital settlement is worked out and things are going along pretty well, introduction to the new significant other seems to starts this process sometimes. Unfortunately, it's not just new male or female friends, quite often it is grandparents. These are people who have had a positive, loving relationship with the child their entire life, but now they become objects of hate. An evaluator will see evidence of a child having a good relationship with grandparents and be very involved through photographs. The separation/divorce will occur at sometime and if PAS is present, suddenly that child will begin to express a real dislike and even hatred of those grandparents because they're the father and the mother of the targeted parent. It goes beyond this as well. The child becomes alienated from ultimately everything in the targeted parent's life. For example, subsequent to a divorce a child who always played soccer, with the father heavily involved - perhaps even as the coach of the team, what sometimes happens is the child suddenly loses interest in playing soccer. They will suddenly start saying things like, "I hate soccer".

The expression of this symptom is not just alienation from people; it can be activities, careers, colors, etc., things commonly associated with the targeted parent. One example is of a targeted parent who was a physician and one of their children who wanted to be a doctor. The child was tracking towards that career choice and abandoned it altogether once the PAS process began to happen. They actually said they hate doctors and they think "that doctors are just into it for the money." The child developed a very different spin that obviously they did not have before.

Symptom Journal
Conceptually it's important to understand that these eight symptoms really operate as a symptom checklist. The evaluator or therapist can then determine the degree of each symptom's presence or absence. The symptom presence will tell you a lot about the development as to how evolved PAS is, if it is present at all. The absence of the symptoms will suggest that the child's behaviors are coming from something else. A genuinely abused child will not present with the PAS symptoms. Please refer to Appendix A for the PA/PAS Journal to be used as a checklist aid in diagnosing and planning treatment for these cases.

Chapter 3: Three Types of Parental Alienation Syndrome

Gardner (1992, 1998) identified three types or levels of severity of PAS. He divided them into a very convenient system that shows the predictable, progressive nature of this problem. The levels were Mild, Moderate and Severe cases. The levels depict the progression of the symptoms in a particular pattern. We are going to look at each symptom and see how they present in children at the different levels and why they work that way. The way we are going to be describing PAS severity levels has the most internal consistency and the greatest degree of predictive value.

Before we get into the first level, the Mild level of PAS, medical science strives to find greater detail, greater discriminations within particular disorders. Years ago Gardner used the example of heart disease. Now there are subtypes of heart disease that help physicians understand the etiology of some of the disorders. Finer categorizations help physicians with treatment. Gardner was trying to create a model of PAS following a more traditional medical approach in the development of PAS by coming up with the levels of Mild, Moderate and Severe. Gardner and others, such as Johnson and Campbell (1988) who wrote the book *Impasses of Divorce: The Dynamics and Resolution of Family Conflict,* had expressed parental conflicts as having a similar foundation. In 1988, Johnson and Campbell introduced the concept of high conflict families and referred to less severe levels of conflict. So, Gardner's levels of severity were his attempt to discriminate among the PAS cases and suggest modes of treatment for each.

The progression of PAS has implications for intervention and treatment. The severity of PAS means interventions have to be vastly different. A common misperception about PAS is once PAS is identified the child has to be removed from an alienating parent and placed with the target parent. This is simply not true of anyone who ever recognized PAS as a legitimate disorder including Gardner and the present authors. The allegation that the authors "find PAS under every rock", is simply not true and quite to contrary have in many cases shown PAS is not present. Only under very specific circumstances changing an alienated child's placement might apply. Antagonists of PAS frequently misstate this position. It is very important to determine whether a case involves Mild, Moderate or Severe alienation to determine the best treatment modality.

Levels of Severity of PAS
If we think of the symptoms of PAS distributed as in a skewed distribution on a graphed "S" curve, the Moderate level intersects the curve in the center dividing the two other levels, with Mild to the left and Severe to the right. Think of the Y Axis as the level of intensity of the symptoms and the X Axis as the number of symptoms. As you move from the Zero point to the right along the X Axis, you will be moving from a Mild level to a Moderate level to a Severe level. As you do so, you will begin to see more of the symptoms present and their intensity increasing. The difference between the levels can be dramatic. The difference between the ranges is vast. It spans from having a few of the symptoms, infrequently, at a low level of intensity, to a more moderate level with symptoms most of the time at a moderate level of intensity and then to be dramatically present in terms of number of symptoms at the highest level of intensity.

Levels of PAS

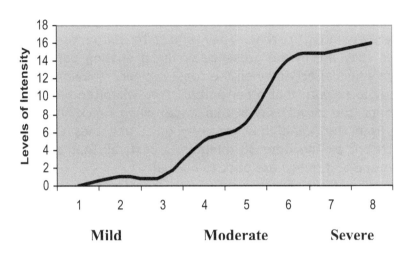

Mild   **Moderate**   **Severe**

Mild Cases of PAS

We begin by looking at Mild cases and the symptoms of the *Campaign of Denigration*, which may or may not include false allegations of abuse.

In Mild cases the symptoms will commonly be observed to be at a fairly minimal level. Children at this level generally come forth with critical things about one parent but it will not be overwhelming or to any dramatic degree. The alienation process will be in its earliest stages when it is the most difficult to diagnose. Therefore, in mild cases the *Campaign of Denigration* will be more than you would expect but won't be overwhelming.

The child at this level of symptom will behave with some ambivalence focused on visitation, a little hesitancy, but there is clearly a present love and affection for the targeted parent. We do not see too much of the angst over visitation as we see in more severe cases.

In this early stage of the process one of the hallmarks of these children, is they will still express affection to the targeted parent. They tend to do it in more restricted ways. They tend to do it when they think word won't get back to the other (alienating) parent. They tend to be a little more stilted when they are in the presence of the alienating parent. But there still is affection when the coast is clear. They are clearly happy to be with that other parent. You will often hear these parents (the target) say at this stage: when I pick him or her up, from the home, they're really quiet and they don't say much but by the time 30 minutes is past, all that aloofness has gone and things are back to normal.

You will not typically see all of the symptoms at this level, only some of them.

The *Weak, Frivolous or Absurd Rationalizations* for the deprecations also occur at a minimal level. This is consistent with the *Campaign of Denigration* being not all that developed yet, so one will hear some negative criticisms but the level of criticisms makes the second symptom, the *Weak, Frivolous, Absurd Rationalizations* for the *Campaign of Denigration* somewhat less and therefore more difficult to pick out because the vilification is so much more minimal.

With the symptom of *Lack of Ambivalence*, for example, it is usually fairly normal. That is, there isn't a lot of ambivalence regarding the targeted parent. Their relationship is fairly normal and consistent. There may be some strained moments here or there. It is like the child is trying to get a sense at how they need to be behaving, both in front of the alienating parent as well as in the presence of the targeted parent alone.

Ambivalence, as we are using the term here, is what every parent knows. Occasionally the child will be very upset with the target parent by saying "It's better at mom's than here" but five- minutes later it is obvious that the positive emotional connection is still present but there remains an ambivalent (love and unsettledness) connection even in the presence of anger.   So, at the mild PAS level one still sees the ambivalence somewhat in operation. It is only when the level of PAS severity increases do we notice the *Lack of Ambivalence* begin to surface more dramatically.

The *Independent Thinking Phenomenon* is usually not present in the Mild level.   There is not a lot to be independently thinking about. If the child doesn't have a lot of negativity directed toward a targeted parent, then they do not have many declarations that the views just expressed are "my own ideas" kind of thing. My own idea at this stage of the process is I still love both of my parents, I feel connected, we still have a relationship and somehow I'm just betting that they'll get back together.   So, typically, we will see that this symptom is not here at this point.

The observable quality of the *Independent Thinker Phenomenon* is a child coming in and saying "You know, no one told me to say this …" and then continue with their complaint about the parent. This behavior logically does not make sense at this particular level because they are simply not saying that many negative things about the target parent. The *Independent Thinker Phenomenon* would only begin to be observed once the *Campaign of Denigration* is more progressed.   All of the symptoms work together and are correlated.

The *Reflexive Support* of the alienating parent in the conflict arena with the parents is observed at this minimal level. This is where the child is not championing, to any great extent, the alienating parent. When we see this symptom at its severest, the child professes that everything the targeted parent is and does is all bad.   The opposite is also observed, that is everything about the alienating parent is all good. Again this will be at a minimal or beginning level in the Mild level, therefore, one might see some one-sided thinking, but it will be at its infancy. The beginning stages may include a general preference for the alienating parent.   It may be possible to pick up which parent is seen as the most powerful at this level. Another way to look at it is which parent the child fears most. In PAS cases, the parent that they tend to side with will be the one that they are fearful of upsetting. The symptom will emerge in little ways in terms of supporting the alienating parent with issues regarding the parental conflicts.

The symptom of *Absence of Guilt* will also be at a minimal level, one will actually be able to observe the child feeling some guilt in terms of the relationship between them and the targeted parent. They will feel badly for that parent. They may express some sympathetic emotions and concern that may dissolve as the level of severity increases. Therapists working with families in this situation will be in an advantageous position to observe the changes in the child's behavior and affect as the severity increases. It will be critical for that therapist to be knowledgeable about this disorder; otherwise, they may make some incorrect assumptions about what is going on in the case.

The way this *Absence of Guilt* will operate is that the child, when they are with the therapist, will tell them things critical of the targeted parent but the child will be very opposed to having those issues brought up when they are sitting in the room with the parent. In other words, they will feel guilty and uncomfortable. While they are willing to say negative things to the therapist, they don't want them to be shared in the presence of that parent. The therapist will begin to see the strains of this developing in that particular way. The therapist needs to tune-in on those kinds of reactions and they can be very instructive.

The *Borrowed Scenarios* symptom, as with the others, because they are not well developed in terms of the denigrations, is going to be at a minimal level. The therapist or evaluator will not see a whole lot of it. This level of PAS is in the very beginning of the indoctrination process, therefore, at a very mild level, hence the category.

In lieu of borrowed scenarios, however, one may begin to see suspiciousness. The suspiciousness is related to the veracity or the truthfulness of the targeted parent. The child may begin to shift in their belief perhaps because the child is beginning to be exposed to two different stories. At this point, especially in the early stages of the divorce process, most children try to stay out of the middle. But with PAS cases, there will be a slight shifting, leaning more one way. Typically it is the parent that they almost always spend the least time with, that they've become the most suspicious of.

The *Spread of the Animosity to the Extended Family* and the friends of the alienated parent is also minimal at this level of PAS. The relationships are usually maintained with grandparents and other relations within that targeted parent's family and so the child feels fairly comfortable at this point. But it is not like there is a total absence of this symptom; you are going to get a sense of this disease that's going on. You will hear a little more protest about going over to see grandma and grandpa where it wasn't there before. "Oh, I don't want to do that – there's nothing to do over there". And that may be a normal response but you hear a little more of that than you did prior to this process. You will begin to see the early stages of this. However, a child that expresses reluctance to visit an extended family member one time is not necessarily displaying this symptom. It has to be a pattern, a general tendency; a change, a shift from how it was before the separation.

An important issue to keep in mind is at this point, there's also an attempt by the child to maintain a positive, healthy relationship with a parent who was the closer bond. Frequently that is the mother. Typically in the early stages of separation and divorce, the children, if they are young will commonly live with the mother; not always, we are seeing a shift, but typically, when people separate it is usually the father that moves out. The children and the mother will typically stay in the marital home. The logistics often are such that it will tend to support this scenario.

As a summary of the Mild level, the transition difficulties for visitation are usually absent or minimal and transitory. The child frequently maintains their relationship with both parents. The behavior during visitation is normal, acceptable and there aren't any major behavior problems that have been fueled. There is a bonding with the alienating parent and that is usually fairly strong and healthy at this stage. One will begin to see attempts to put the targeted parent in a peripheral role in the family by the other parent. On the legal side, you will begin to see problems with visitation. You will begin to see visitation that is not being kept at the hand of the alienating parent. There will be moves to block the visitation and you will start to possibly see injunctions being filed. A therapist may begin to notice the alienation process showing up in other ways. The targeted parent may come into their office, even though their children are still connected to them, and start telling the therapist about visitations that didn't happen. As the process of alienation matures, the therapist will begin to see other symptoms cropping up. A pattern may emerge; a beginning of an imbalance. It is beginning to tip just a little bit this way or that way. Like most disease processes, it is most difficult to detect in the earlier stages, but if it is caught early, it can be extremely advantageous to the children, as opposed to trying to address it later on.

Moderate Cases of PAS
At the Moderate level of PAS the symptoms start to increase in frequency and intensity. At this stage one may see at least six or seven, if not all eight, of the symptoms. Gardner would argue that you will see all eight symptoms.

So if we look at the *Campaign of Denigration*, this has now ratcheted up to a much more involved level. Here the child is being a lot more vocal about their dislike, hatred and the faults of the targeted parent. There are problems with the relationship between the child and the targeted parent. The *Campaign of Denigration* typically is what most people can recognize at the Moderate level. In its scope the Moderate level presents a wide ranging spectrum of symptoms, definitely more than we saw before. There is a theme being developed that the child will bring up in an unsolicited way when they are in a therapist's office. The reason this surfaces at this point in time is because this is where we start to see visitation problems. This is also a typical time people are establishing relationships with attorneys and they may or may not seek out a mental health professional. It is at this point that things become much more visible. There is a system of sorts progressing here. The system is progressing to the point where this is now going to demand attention.

Just as the accusations have increased to a threshold level, we now have the same *Weak, Frivolous and Absurd Rationalizations* for those deprecations also reaching a threshold level. The child is much more verbal about their disdain for the targeted parent, but their arguments and rationales for that distain are not really credible or substantiated.

Here the PAS process really begins to show up most clearly. It is in the combination of these two symptoms at this point. Now the child is saying clearly things like "I don't want to go see (the targeted parent), I don't like them", etc. When asked, what do you mean, this is your mother or father, what did she/he do? There will be, first of all pauses, then "I don't know, I just don't like her/him". Next you will begin to hear responses of made up or small things that have happened, their significance exaggerated and blown up well beyond their original level. An example might be a parent was a few minutes late coming home from work and the child will tell the other parent that the parent left them alone with no further details provided. The impression will be that the parent was totally absent from the child for an extended period. So the child will argue that they don't like visiting that parent because the parent is never there. This is a significantly different presentation than in the Mild level.

This now becomes a theme that doesn't make a lot of sense. A clinician who is naive about this will ask themselves and others "what happened here"? If they don't know the dynamics of PAS, they will think, something bad must have happened between this child and this parent, when in actual fact all the evidence suggests the targeted parent and child had a very good relationship. Now there has been this change, without any clear reason or any precedent for the change.

With *Lack of Ambivalence* we are starting to see the absence of any kind of ambivalence in terms of the relationships. These children are very clear, Mom or Dad (the target parent) is all bad and the other parent (favored parent) is all good. Since this is a process, you will begin to see the ambivalence not just suddenly evaporate but it will begin to slowly go away. Clearly, there is less good, if anything, that they can say at all about the targeted parent. If you bring out photographs of life before divorce and ask them to talk about them, they will have very little to say or they will say that they were faking it, or they had to do that or the targeted parent would beat them, etc. In one recent case a child actually has asked her father if she could live with him. Less than two years later her father was considered abusive and someone she didn't want anything to do with. When reminded by an evaluator that she stated she wanted to live with the father, she could remember making the statement but couldn't explain why she changed her mind or what happened; it's just that she heard that he is abusive; no other explanation was forthcoming. So when you begin to see this symptom clearly develop, the case could be in the Moderate stage.

It is important also to point out that when you take out those photographs, the obvious contradiction to their position is now coming up with these excuses; I was faking it, I didn't really mean to smile, etc... As you begin to present these questions in a way that reveals that contradiction, you will see the therapeutic relationship cool off. What we have noticed is that the children will begin to realize they are being challenged to justify or explain why they feel the way that they do. So

-44-

depending on what your role is in the case, such as a therapist or GAL, when you start asking these questions, you will hear the child say things like "you're not helping", or you'll begin to hear resistance from the alienating parent before and after a session, or there will be missed appointments, or people will not call back unless they are court ordered, etc…

When asked straight away if they have ever had a good time with this parent, have they ever had a good relationship, the answer is no, never!

It is in the Moderate Level of PAS where we see *The Independent Thinker Phenomenon* evolve. The child professes that "these are my ideas and nobody told me to say this, nobody put me up to this." Frequently this will be proclaimed even in the absence of being asked "Did anyone tell you to say that." We have experienced a number of children coming in for the first time, sitting down and announcing "nobody told me to say this, but you need to know my father … (fill in the blank, is abusive, hits me, abandoned me, etc.)". The motivation for this proclamation is obviously they have either an unconscious unstated sense that someone may think that someone did tell them or consciously were reciting a prerecorded script.

In the *Reflective Support* of an alienating parent, consistent with all the other symptoms, is where the child cannot find anything good about the targeted parent. The targeted parent is viewed as not having done anything right relative to the parental conflict or the divorce. In other words, if you ask the child, "Do you side with your Dad on any of these things that come up?" they will say, "Absolutely not". Whereas in divorce, where PAS is not present, you will typically see children be able to endorse a position taken by one parent and then endorse the other parent in another issue or set of issues. The normal response of children in divorce is to try to stay out of the middle. In PAS what you see is the child taking on the responsibility to resolve the conflict, by taking a definite, unambiguous side. This becomes more obvious when the process has moved into the Moderate stage.

In the *Absence of Guilt* there is either minimal or no guilt whatsoever. If there is any guilt it is at a minimum level and will soon evaporate to none at all. The absence of guilt is in terms of putting the other parent down, the suffering that parent may be experiencing because of the lack of their relationship with the child. If the targeted parent expresses love and caring for that child and missing them there is no real warm response or empathy. In one case an adolescent blankly looked at this grandfather who was pleading with him to tell the grandfather what he had done to be abandoned by his grandson. The boy was emotionless, while everyone else in the room was tearing-up.

The absence of guilt, remorse, empathy doesn't just suddenly go away like flipping a switch. It is something that normally erodes over time. What is observable, however is the child taking a different position than previously; a change or shift in their orientation. You will see the child not be moved by the other parent's suffering, which is typically not present in cases without PAS. This is one of the symptoms that when you begin to see this, you are more deeply into the syndrome.

In *Borrowed Scenarios* you will hear the same vocabulary, the same arguments coming from the child as you hear from the alienating parent. One clue maybe the vocabulary might even be beyond the developmental level of the child. At times you will hear young children using words like 'harassing' as in "he harasses us". When you ask the child what the word means, they simply don't know. You'll also hear the pairing in your words, "he divorced us; he left us". This is similar to a kind of affiliation and a squaring off of sides in the dispute and is reflective of a kind of enmeshed relationship that happens between a child and the alienating parent. Frequently you will hear the inappropriate use of the first person plural when they ought to be using the first person singular, 'we' instead of 'I'.

When you hear a four or five-year old child say "I don't feel safe", that's not a concept a child this age typically articulates.

The *Spread of Animosity for the Extended Family of the Alienated Parent* is observable at this level. This also includes other people and activities normally associated with the target parent. You will see where the child is being programmed to dislike the targeted parent's parents, the grandparents, and clearly, if there is a stepparent involved, they are very easy targets as well. In the Mild cases this is minimally present, but now at this stage it is clearly present. This, like the other symptoms, is represented in the change or shift from before the divorce or separation experience of the child and to what is presently going on.

Regardless of your role in these cases, whether at the Severe level or the Moderate level, a very important thing to do, is look for evidence of these symptoms, characteristics and complaints prior to the separation. Typically in cases where PAS is operating you will see evidence of a prior good relationship or at a minimum not a bad one. Also, there will be the ever increasing incidents of visitation difficulties and difficulties during transition time. You will see a child refusing to go see a target parent. There will be reports of behavior problems during visitation. In one case we had a 12-year-old actually having temper tantrums with the father and the stepmother and it has surfaced within the last year; since the father remarried. There are strong to moderate levels of pathology. It is common to see unhealthy bonding and an enmeshment between the alienating parent and child with the bonding between the targeted parent and child starting to erode.

The most tell-tale sign is the bonding with the alienating parent and the child; they are virtually joined at the hip. Professionals in the case will learn that the child is sleeping with the alienating parent with multiple excuses, commonly blaming the targeted parent, as to why they are doing so. At the Moderate stage, even though there are problems with visitation and at times behavior, there still is some sort of a bond between the child and the targeted parent. This may sound strange since with the child is demonstrating a *lack of ambivalence* but sometimes you will see evidence of a relationship. It is evidenced by the affect the child demonstrates in the presence of the targeted parent that is inconsistent with all the things that they have said about them. It may be subtle, but there is still some sense of connectedness present. Recall our earlier discussion regarding the primary psychological bond very strong with both parents and the child. It is not easy to alienate a child from a parent; it takes a lot of work for the bond to be completely broken. We begin to observe what we call the "rear view mirror" phenomenon. This is where as the house of the alienating parent disappears out of the rear view mirror, then so does some of the symptomatology of the PAS. That is, this is when the child's resistance of the visitation starts to wear off. After a few blocks from the alienating parent, the child and targeted parent are back to a relatively normal relationship.

Professionals may listen to this strange experience the targeted parent describes as to how they are treated by the child. Generally they are treated terribly and had terrible things said to them but as soon as they get away together away from the alienating parent, then their relationship changes for the better. Then on their return to the alienating parent they tend to freeze up and become aloof and separate again. A daughter tells her father over the telephone "it's none of your business" and hangs up in response to the father asking "what's going on there?" Later when the child is with the father during visitation he asks what her response was all about. She stated, "oh sorry, I just had some friends over".

Professionals in a case will hear the hypothesis that the child doesn't want to go back to the alienating parent, but it is their resistance to leave that will be presented as "see they don't want to even go back to the alienating parent". The reality is this is really a way for the child to get prepared for the

-48-

transition again to demonstrate to the alienating parent "I had a terrible time with him, you're right, he's really a bad person or she's a bad person and I really want to stay with you". They want to reestablish the bond, to strengthen the bond, with the alienating parent. They have to get back into character.

Children where PAS is operating have to assume multiple roles in their relationships with the parents. A child's image of the targeted parent shifts after a good visitation and the truthful model of their parent resurfaces in their mind; a sort of reminder of the positive characteristics of their parent. The positive qualities are reinforced and fed by their contact during the visitation. But when the child is preparing to return to the alienating parent, they have to retrieve the image of the target parent, they have to put on the other mask in order to be consistent, lest they will be criticized or even abandoned by the alienating parent.

Severe Cases of PAS
Obviously as the name suggests, we are talking about a significant increase in the symptoms, the intensity and frequency that one is going to experience with this level of PAS takes a dramatic turn. The *Campaign of Denigration* is probably hard to believe if one has not experienced any of these cases at this level. One cannot imagine how horrible some of the things that are being said and done to the targeted parent that is just beyond one's imagination in some cases. This is very uncommon, even in cases of adversarial divorces. The default setting for children whose parents are divorcing when there is no PAS is to not want to take sides with either parent. So to see this level of pathology is really different. Gardner described this as formidable. It's a fanatical level of a *campaign of denigration* where a child will expend a tremendous amount of time enumerating all the horrible things that have happened to them at the hand of the target parent. Frequently children, because they've been through this so many times before, will sit there and one can see them mentally going down a bullet point list of all the

horrible things that have happened and why they don't want to see that parent. You can see them look up at the ceiling to retrieve more information, then look at the therapist, GAL, evaluator, etc... and begin again "there was this time ...". They will start talking about something and then become more animated because what they were talking about triggered something that was more real to their experience. Then they will remember something else and say "oh, wait a minute, hold it, I just thought about something else". They will tell you some other experiences or some other reasons why they don't want to see the other parent and how much they can't stand them. There is just a very distinctly different quality to the children's behavior relative to this problem. In one case the child had not seen the father for several months because of an injunction filed against him and at the same time there was a break in the child's therapy sessions also for several months. When the therapy resumed, the child simply brought up all the old complaints to the therapist, because of the hiatus in visits with the parent the child didn't have anything new to complain about.

Now, if you think about what a professional involved in a case who doesn't know about PAS might respond with when this child comes in presenting all this, it's very moving. It is the kind of thing that if a GAL is appointed in a case and a child says this, that Guardian who doesn't understand PAS might suggest getting an injunction to prevent further visits. If the police are called out to someone's house and a child says this to a police officer, the police officer might try to arrest the person the child was referring to and they perhaps weren't even there. If no arrest is made, the police officer will likely advise the parent to go to court and get an injunction or a restraining order. So you can see the roll that the child plays in this which later damages their self-esteem because at some level they realize that none of this is true.

This is where Gardner (1998) suggested that we consider the shared psychotic delusion diagnosis. It is at a severe pathological level at this point. So the *campaign of denigration* is extreme in terms of what kinds of things are being said, how frequently they're being done and their intensity. There is this intense preoccupation with the negativity that just doesn't exist in the other levels within the PAS spectrum and doesn't typically exist in most divorce cases. Some would argue that this degree of adversarial conflict typically exists in high conflict divorce cases. Gardner would not disagree with that, but we're talking about looking at this in conjunction with the other symptoms to see that this is really moving more toward a common cluster of symptoms where there is a *primary* etiology or source as is found in syndromes. The word primary is emphasized because we recognize the target parent almost always plays a role, but not even close to the role the alienating parent does.

In our experience, even in very high conflict divorce situations there is no campaign to alienate one parent from the children by the other parent. Children may have complaints about one or both parents, or maybe even predominantly about one, but that won't be the main focus they want to talk about. They will want to talk about other issues going on and they will almost avoid talking about their parents but they will respond to questions. The siding with one of the parents, however, will not be leading edge of the message they want to deliver. With children in PAS cases it is very different. One gets the sense they're trying to convince you how horrible this other parent is and that is really very unusual.

The *Weak, Frivolous or Absurd Rationalizations*, as one might expect, increase in frequency and absurdity. As the list of complaints increases, the reasons behind those complaints also rise, but in an absurd manner. Absurd is the right word. We have had, especially with younger children; descriptions of things that just frankly violate the laws of physics, about how certain things could happen. One of the most common, by the way, is especially if the mother is the targeted parent, you'll hear a child describe the mother as having picked them up and strangled them. Actually, this would be more of a different symptom but still the absurdity of it – strangle them.

Strangle them and lift them off the ground so their feet are dangling, holding them by the neck. You'll hear it from a child who weighs the same as the parent, if not more. In another case, the ten-year old child claimed the father put a belt around his neck, but he pushed him away, thereby preventing the father from strangling him.

We recently had a case where the Dad is about 4'8" and the son is 6'5". The mother actually took out a complaint against the father because he was physically abusive to the child and the father just said, "look at me, this kid could pound me into the ground, it's just like no way; it just can't happen".

Generally speaking, a good rule of thumb: if things sound like they aren't likely to occur, then probably they didn't happen. If it's hard to believe, it's probably not believable.

Regardless of the likelihood, these events require investigation but it is important that one step back and look at what's really being said; frequently something a court does not always do. Courts and GALs will tend to focus only on what the child says and will not critique it. It is an old traditional thought process that if a child says something it must be true. So that's one of the biggest problems in dealing with how one plans the interventions to this and we'll get to that at a later point.

In the *Lack of Ambivalence* the child is clearly entrenched in one direction; there is no ambivalence. They know who the good person is and they know who the bad one is and no amount of convincing evidence will change that. There are no recollections of good times or happy times. The targeted parent is all bad and that's all there is to it.

No amount of hypothetical questions designed to get a child's affect will bring any kind of an emotional response. When asked "what if your father was dead?" "What if you have terminal disease?" "What if you had it and he gave you his kidney because you had kidney disease?" "Would that change your mind?" There is nothing, regardless of how one tries to create a hypothetical question for these children that bring some sort of an emotional response, it's just not there. You can't get it.

This is very unusual. If the hatred was there by virtue of true actual abuse, there would have to be so much of it, that it would be clearly demonstrable and documented. Victimized children who are victims of their parent's abuse really want their parents just to be good parents. They don't want them absent from their lives. That is the opposite of what we are seeing here.

The *Independent Thinker Phenomenon* is clearly present. The anti-parent position is the child's idea and nobody put them up to it. We know of a case where some adolescent boys are just so anti-mother, it's just unbelievable and they are treating her in such a despicable manner and according to them no one put them up to this; this is their idea. She, their mother is just this horrible, terrible woman and yet there's documentation to prove how involved she was when they were younger children.

In cases like these, typically the children are older adolescents who very often have a secondary gain for maintaining portrayed hatred. We're recalling a case where there were a number of children and the mother was the targeted parent. Even when the children reached ages of majority, when you would expect them not to be under the sway of the alienating parent, they still were espousing their hatred. Well it turns out in this particular case, and in others, there was a huge pay-off by the alienating parent to the children in the form of money in the millions of dollars and expensive cars; absence of that information, their behavior was hard to explain.
There comes a point where the alienation is so thorough that the parent-child bonds are completely corrupted and broken; the delusion becomes reality.

In the *Absence of Guilt,* the child displays absolutely no guilt or remorse at all. The state of affairs is the way it is, it's justified and there is a rationale, a justification for their feelings toward that targeted parent. No one is going to sway them.

Think about what guilt means. Guilt is an emotion that is tied to empathy and conscience. It is tied to moderating self-behavior. If guilt is absent over cruelty to the targeted parent, it creates a severe disorder in that child. This is one of the most critical elements of this. If one of the sources of your superego, leaning a little bit toward psychodynamic/psychoanalytic perspective, is now considered a villain in your life and not a person of guidance it creates a huge disorder that will stay with you and very likely follow you the rest of your life once it gets entrenched.

With *Borrowed Scenarios* by the child, at this level of PAS, they present with a virtually verbatim presentation of the alienating parent. It is just stronger, more prevalent and very obvious. At this point, however, one typically sees the alienating parent say almost nothing. They don't have to. They step back and it looks like the ball has been handed off. Often they will take the position, and this could be also true in the Moderate level as well, that "Gee, I've been trying to get them to warm up to their mother/father but what am I going to do, they don't want to be with them, it's their choice".

Spread of Animosity to the Extended Family, as one would imagine is formable. It is frequent and it's fanatical. These are the cases where you will see a child express hatred for the grandparents, when there was evidence that they previously had a good relationship with them. It's not uncommon to have the grandparents at some later time be accused of having sexually molested the child. What typically also follows is where the targeted parent is commonly accused falsely of sexually molesting a child and often the accusations will shift to a grandparent because grandparents are often used in childcare, especially when children are very young.

Also this will happen especially if the grandparents are trying to help to correct the situation. They may be doing so in the form of paying for legal fees, counseling and so forth. So they'll get drawn into the situation, targeted and punished by virtue of their involvement.

It is heart wrenching to watch one of these things progress in this manner. Those who work in the forensic field and work with the legal system, know how slow the system moves and how these situations are worsened because of the slowness of the system to respond. We'll talk about that later but the speed, or lack thereof in the legal system is one of the key elements in these cases; it is really tragic to watch these dramas unfold.

We'll see significant visitation problems, if there are any visits at all. Very frequently, visits have stopped with the excuse that the child doesn't want to go, it is their choice and the favored parent is not going to force them. At this stage of the PAS process there has been no visitation, sometimes for a very long time, in some of our cases for years! The reasons given for the child's absence are related to the horrible things done to the children when they are with that parent. The alienating parent claims the children need protection and therefore cannot go to the other parent's residence. In many cases this is the time injunctions are put in place with allegations of sexual abuse, physical abuse and neglect. In the PAS process this often starts out with an abuse allegation in some form against the targeted parent and then the allegation expands. It frequently starts out with accusations of emotional abuse. If that doesn't keep the child away from the other parent it escalates to "he is also physically abusive". If that doesn't work the next allegation to come around will be an allegation of the children having been sexually abused. If one allegation of sexual or physical abuse doesn't work, there commonly are others repeating the claims. Many of the subsequent complaints happen even in the absence of contact with the target parent and the visits have been interrupted for some time. It is not unusual for PAS cases to have four or five reported incidents of abuse levied against a target parent with Child Protection agencies investigating a parent numerous times, with multiple police investigations and no one is accountable.

The targeted parent is in the difficult position of proving him or herself innocent instead of being proven guilty. The punishment is immediate removal of the child from their life. Only after the punishment has been administered will there be a hearing to determine if the claims are valid. Interestingly enough when all the evidence is in, the decision is that the charges could not be proven; not that the target parent is innocent. It is noteworthy as well to observe that the parent alleging abuse gets totally away without any consequences. Frequently, even the missed time with a parent is not even made up.

This is where the child now starts to act out, often because of the frustration of this whole situation. It's not the alienating parent's fault because they are really well defended; it is always somebody else's fault. We have heard from attorneys who say "what if you're dealing with adolescents". These are common issues that surface when you are dealing with a teenager. They have their own lives and seek to be independent anyway. At this point, adolescents socialize with their own peer group and it becomes more of a choice of who they want to spend their time with. Going to visit the other parent is sort of "old hat". Anybody who has dealt with visitation issues in post-divorce situations knows that the visitation patterns do change when children become teenagers. But in cases where PAS is going on one finds that normal human behavior seems to accelerate and intensify. One needs to conceptually segregate the adolescent from other children of divorce who are refusing to visit and are exhibiting other symptoms. It is not convenient for the normal adolescent, who is busy with the football, baseball, soccer, dance, etc..., to visit the other parent. However, they will not necessarily have negative things to say about the other parent. It's just that they're not fitting the visits into their schedule.

So if one observes any one of the symptoms being at a severe level and the others are not, then this may be an indication that PAS may not be going on. These symptoms work together in concert and they really are all highly correlated in a very logical way. There be a child who, instead of visiting a parent, wants to go out-of-town to play softball with their team. The targeted parent doesn't want them to do that and the child complains about it or balks about the visit. That is not an indication that PAS is operating in this case. It may just be a stubborn parent who misinterprets what's best for the child.

This can become an issue for counseling for that parent. They need to understand children's developmental levels and psychological needs. This could be an issue for a counselor, a parenting coordinator or even an attorney where the parent needs to hear "you know you need to maintain a relationship here. This is what you have to do. You have to meet this child half-way. You go to the softball game". These parents often misinterpret timesharing and think that the time with their child is their time, meaning the parent's time. Actually it's the child's time with the parent. It's not the other way around and that's what these parents have to learn.

The major point here too is that in severe PAS cases we're looking at significant pathology between a child and the alienating parent. It is a very important issue. At this stage of the PAS process there is now a total enmeshment between alienating parent and child. It is not unusual in these cases to hear of children as old as 12-year-old, and even older, who are sleeping in their mother's bed. Often you see those things happen, especially with sleeping and doing things that you wouldn't expect a child of that age to still be doing (e.g., sucking thumbs, wetting themselves, etc...). And more often than not, when it is closely investigated, you find that it is the child that's doing it for the parent's benefit.

Differentiating Between Genuine and False Abuse Claims

As stated earlier, in cases of actual abuse children will typically try to maintain a relationship with an abusing parent. So, it's relatively unusual for a child to pull away from, be alienated and not have contact at all with that parent. Children may try to avoid certain situations, but it is unusual for them to exhibit total avoidance of an abusive parent. This attachment frequently continues into adult dysfunctions such as seeking out and maintaining abusive relationships.

As an example of a child's devotion to their parents, there was an abuse case where a law enforcement officer described the scene when he arrested a suspected perpetrator of child abuse. During a visit to an alcoholic parent a child was burned by cigarettes and had fresh burn marks on their arm. When the police arrived and arrested the parent responsible the child tearfully protested the arrest! So we know, considering the very powerful bond that exists between parents and children, it takes a tremendous amount of abuse to create a fully alienated child. We have seen adults who were the victims of child abuse and still some of the most powerful people in their lives emotionally are their abusive parent. As adults they may have learned to avoid them, learned to erect boundaries to protect themselves, but it was not their natural tendency; they had to learn a healthier way to have a relationship. Their natural inclination was to still try to somehow please that abusive parent. As adults, abused children may decide to sever ties with an abusive parent but not when they are children. In PAS cases it is really very much the opposite.

Hypothesizing why a child is demonstrating alienating behaviors may be a challenge to evaluators, therapists, parenting coordinators and even attorneys in a case. Typically there is not an abundance of evidence of abuse. There frequently are no police reports, hospital records, witnesses or collateral informants describing abusive acts. The alienating parent will give some details and situational

-58-

accounts of abuse. The children may echo some of this information but will frequently be contradictory in what one would expect in the presence of abuse that is being reported to an evaluator.

This distinction is very important to keep in mind because in PAS cases children can exhibit high levels of alienation allegedly stemming from abuse. Given the degree of abuse that is typically expressed it shouldn't be difficult to find evidence of real abuse. In one trial where Richard Gardner was testifying, he was asked by an attorney, "how much abuse would it take before a child would have this level of alienation?" Dr. Gardner said "severe, acute and chronic physical abuse whereby there would be police reports, there would be emergency room visits, there would be broken bones, there would be things like that – that level of abuse to warrant this level of alienation."

So considering our earlier discussion about the effects of abuse on children, it becomes a little easier to determine PAS from other forms of parental alienation. "A little easier" may be somewhat misleading. Sometimes this is not easy to do at all and it takes quite a bit of effort and investigation. If one goes into a case with filters on that suggests PAS does not exist, that person is biased and will not find it regardless of the quantity of evidence. The best clinicians are the ones who advocate for the children looking at what is in their best interests. A bias for or against anything is not in the best interests of the children. Having an open mind in an investigation, through in-depth inquires, evaluations and treatment supports the children and parents.

Because clinicians have been trained to meet clients where they are, that is, unconditional positive regard, especially with children, they are inclined not to question what they are saying. If a child comes in claiming to be fearful of a parent, frequently the default position is to believe them and address their fears and the target of their fears. However, in cases where PAS is operating it is a disservice to that child to completely accept their overt claims and behavior. Analyzing and uncovering a PAS situation is very different for most clinicians to consider, because it is an exception to the unconditional positive regard rule.

Another important point in uncovering PAS is the behavior of the alienating parent which is rather telling as well. In a healthy relationship, a parent recognizes and understands the real value of a child having both parents involved in that child's life. The healthy stance is to typically foster the positive relationship with the other parent. Even in the most strained of divorce relationships you will find the children having some contact with the other parent. In cases with PAS you don't find that encouragement. Children don't have contact with the targeted parent. There is virtually no recognition that it's good for the children to be involved with both parents. There is frequently a denial of any of the above, especially in the case of PAS because the alienating person is so abusive, neglectful and hurtful.

Chapter 4: Child's Underlying Psychodynamics

It might be helpful to consider the children's underlying psycho-dynamics that occur in the process of PAS. That is, what happens to the child psychologically and what is going on?

A good backdrop might be a concept that the authors developed a number of years ago. In our metaphor, human development was compared to a jukebox. We are reminded, however, that given the 21st Century some readers may have not seen or heard of a jukebox or records and if they did it was probably in a museum. So this metaphor will be updated to consider the workings of a computer. Computers have an operating system that essentially takes input from a user and then translates that input into specific digital operations. The typical non-technical computer user doesn't see or manipulate the functioning of the operating system. It functions completely below our awareness. Operating systems also control application software, which takes a user's input and produces a specific result, such as a word processing application. So, using this metaphor, let's say from the time you are born, your operating system is taking in the input of your experiences through your senses. This is where we start to create files that help us operate in this world in both the short term and long term. We make files about ourselves that effect how we behave and interact in our relationships. We develop a sense of self: Am I lovable? Am I attractive? Am I competent? When a child watches his or her mother they learn what it is like to be a woman, a mother and a wife. When a child watches his or her father they learn what it is like to be a man, a husband and a father. The observations and interactions of the child create the impressions the child stores. The impressions saved are not necessarily accurate documentaries of those observations and interactions. All through childhood and into adulthood people, events, situations push their "buttons" and what do they do? The operating system plays the files that were recorded and installed earlier, i.e., the impressions. We play the only files and programs we have, even though they are below our awareness. Conceptually, from about eight or nine-years old, the basic program files have been installed. So as an adult we experience life situations and experience different emotions which are based on what was installed when we were young. Certain events during our lives can corrupt our files, such as traumatic events, that distort our files; further distorting our impressions.

Professionals in divorce cases see people and couples in relationships. It is important to understand we also have programs and files that influence our perceptions of the world. Being aware of one's own triggers and biases is important. Frequently in custody cases our impressions regarding PAS can be inaccurate. The phrase "things are never what they appear to be" is good to keep in mind while working with these cases.

Many people tend to believe that memory is like a tape recorder (oh, another old analogy). Research shows, however that memory is a constructed, interactive process rather than simply a passive recording. One way to explain this is to consider that when you think or visualize about the future, about an experience that has not happened, it is the same physiological processes that are used in the construction of the memory of actual events. In divorce cases, with major changes happening to a family, there is a template of some loss, anger, disappointment, etc... that can be filled in or edited and new constructed versions supplied so that a child can then begin to believe something actually occurred.

We know that children are basically egocentric. That is, young children think that the things that are happening in their world are caused by them or could have been prevented by them. So with this backdrop, we look at some of the issues in terms of a child involved in a PAS situation and what they may be bringing to that situation in terms of their psychodynamics.

The model presented above is a way to easily explain human development to clients as well as to judges in court. In one case an attorney told us "most judges are pretty much meat and potato people. This whole business about alienation is a French sauce. So, many times PAS isn't chosen off the menu nor is it digested by the judiciary." It's important to be able to summarize and put in simple terms the concepts of PAS. The model that is being described in this book is a simple way to do that. As workers in this field, it is good to remember to keep things simple and easy to understand. When PAS is in "full bloom", these children are having corrupted files installed; making impressions that will serve as reference points later in their lives. The age of the child as well as when the alienation process begins can have implication as to how the PAS process can manifest itself. One can follow the progression fairly well and see how it could affect them later in life. So the model is a way to explain a lot of these things.

One of the major issues for children is maintaining the primary psychological bond. Children start out bonding very early first to their mothers and then quickly to their fathers. These bonds become something that is incredibly important for the child in order for them to feel safe and trusting in life. These bonds become very close and strong and are normally maintained throughout the child's life. Any disruption to these bonds is going to meet with a lot of resistance, particularly on an unconscious level, because humans have a very delicate and deliberate way of developing mentally and emotionally. When a child enters into an alienation process, where one parent is trying to brainwash and program with the intention to break that bond, that child is going to experience a fear. The child will feel unsafe, become dependent and become fearful not trusting other relationships. If there is an alienating parent trying to alienate the child away from the other parent, that child is going to be resistant to breaking that bond. They will gravitate to counter the alienation tactics. It is going to be very difficult to emotionally separate the child from a parent. Gardner (1998) proposed that it is easier for a mother to engage in an alienation process because of the bond between the mother and child as opposed to the bond between a father and child. The bond with a child's mother is the first bond and a strong bond until later in a child's life when they bond more fully to the father. This is not suggesting fathers do not alienate their children because of a weaker bond; they do. That's why it's important for a father to be present and available to make the beginning connections when their children are young.

In the 1980's and 90's the predominance of parents who were determined to be alienating parents were women. Dr. Gardner was a psychiatrist. Psychiatrists then, were primarily Freudian based in theory and this view of the bonding process fit their theory of psychodynamics. Richard Gardner was criticized deeply for this view and in fact still is, even though posthumously. In 2000 he tried to change that perception. Basically he said there is roughly an equal distribution now between alienating mothers and fathers. However the primary psychological bond is usually with the mother. It would stand to reason that it would make it a little easier task for the mother to become the alienating and ultimately the successful alienating parent than the father.

To be very clear, the research isn't about hypothesizing that women are the predominant alienating parent. As was just stated, even Gardner (2000) had retracted that position and made reference to an equal distribution of alienators between mothers and fathers. It is really important that people hear that we are not saying that women are the primary alienating parents. It is interesting that in spite of all these observations and corrections based on the demographic changes, the critics of PAS are still leveling the same criticisms, which have not been founded in research for many years.

Relative to the bonding process, you will hear that PAS is a fear driven dynamic. The fear has to do with loss. Specifically, in cases when children have become alienated from one parent by actions of another parent, in the child's mind they have lost one parent already. The possibility of losing the other parent drives them to distort their behavior. The alienation disrupts their normal sense of safety and survival, and replaces it with a fear-based survival mode. This reaction serves to modify their behavior in subtle and not so subtle ways. PAS is a fear driven syndrome and a lot of the psychopathology is that of a fear driven type.

A professional working with these cases may hear children report that they are fearful of their mother's reaction if they express any kind of love or caring toward the targeted parent. It is the fear of losing that important psychological bond that the professionals need to be acutely aware of in these cases.

Reaction Formation
Another underlying psychodynamic element that is possible is a reaction formation, where the child will start to use the defense to protect themselves from the fear. Often the obsessive hatred of the targeted parent is a disguise for a continuing loving, affectionate bond for that targeted parent. It's important for professionals in this area to keep an open mind and view the expressed anger and negative feelings expressed by the child as a possible reaction formation defense. That is, a child who obsesses over their hatred of a parent is expending a lot of psychic energy directed toward that parent. If the child and parent's relationship was over, it is more likely the child would experience indifference and not hatred. Maintaining hatred allows a child (or adult) to stay connected to the object of hate. Expressing hatred is a way for a child to maintain the presence of that parent in their life. The parent moves from an object of love to being an object of hate, they remain an object. It's important to rule out the reasons for these behaviors and be able to see past the manifest, or the observable appearance. Professionals may misperceive a child's behavior by taking it on face value and assume there are legitimate grounds for the child's orientation. The legal system, judges and lawyers do not really understand reaction formation so if a child says they hate someone, those in the legal system have difficulty understanding that what is being expressed may just be the

opposite. Because the opposite of love is not hate, it is indifference that is why it's important to look for the possibility of a reaction formation.

Identification
In the identification process children tend to identify initially with their parents. When one parent assumes the role of alienator, they simultaneously take on the role of an aggressor. The child, in an attempt to adjust to this change, actually seeks protection from this aggressor by identifying with them. It's important to remember that the programs/files for this have been installed and then activated when needed; establishing what might become a long-term psychopathology.

If this happens early on, where a child has not developed their own program files, they have the corrupted files created by the aliening parent. Now the child has a file that is similar to a file with a virus of the alienating parent viewing the targeted parent. The child may not have many files created by positive interactions with the targeted parent. Another way to think about this is when a parent has a positive, normal, relationship with their child; the child creates files based on their experiences with input from all their senses. Those experiences and memories form the model (impressions) of who that parent is in that child's mind. However, when the child is separated from that parent and is giving input of untruths about that parent, the child begins to construct a different model (impressions) of that parent. Essentially the child is now faced with two contradictory models of the targeted parent. Certainly there is some of this in any kind of divided loyalty and any divorce, but in the context of PAS it is taken to an extreme. After a while the child, in the absence of the targeted parent, tends to overlay the newly constructed model over the one that was based on actual memories and experiences.

The child becomes basically "brainwashed" or the files (impressions) are corrupted and essentially if there was a

-66-

prior program it is now "damaged". This brings in the issue of memory. How is it that a child can claim to remember things that didn't happen but will do so with such credibility and certainty that it really causes one to pause and wonder if it didn't really happen? We have seen adults take polygraph tests and basically forget the first version of the story they tell and come up with a second version and it is all presented as true.

If our metaphor holds, the child who is building program files using their experiences will experience some disappointments in the relationship, thinking that they may have caused the break. This is a normal and natural response in children whose parents are getting divorce. Children frequently believe that they were the cause of the parent's divorce.

In a PAS context, however, remove the targeted parent and the alienating parent overrides previous messages relative to the child's relationship with the target parent. The alienating parent is the abuser. The targeted parent is an abandoner. And since no parent is perfect, mistakes are always being made. Parents make errors of judgment all the time, some of them are acts without thinking, others are caused by poor skills. From these errors and foibles children create memories; memories of loss or abandonment by a target parent.

As the child overrides previous files that were created, with the help of the alienating parent, their perception is that they caused the disappointment in their relationship; they caused these things to happen. The child's perception becomes further confused by the alienating parent helping to override their memory with statements and situations of abuse, neglect, abandonment, and so on about the targeted parent. The child's egocentricity is still there. The child is reinforced into thinking they created the problem. What is happening is the creation of a personality disorder, a severe psychopathology that wasn't there before.

Everyone creates programs and files from their thoughts about things. That is why when people's buttons are pushed people respond in both positive and negative ways. This analogy isn't just in the context of PAS or isn't just true for divorcing parents. This model is for everyone. It is possible to delete files and to add "healthy" program files. From a conscious, cognitive perspective one could learn to realize, "You know, I made that up. That really didn't happen. That was my story. Those are my beliefs not facts."

Children's Testimony

Dr. Stephen Ceci is well known for his work in the reliability of children's testimony. Children's testimony is connected to children's "memories". Frequently these memories involve being abused. In his workshops he presents case after case of children who have "created a reality or a story" and will go to their grave believing that their false memory is absolutely accurate. These children believe that these experiences have occurred when in fact they could not have occurred. They didn't exist. These memories were completely manufactured.

We have had cases where a parent has been accused of sexual abuse because the child implied an abusive event had occurred. In one case a father was prevented from seeing his 13-year-old daughter because the daughter felt uncomfortable and her behavior had some suggestions that prior sexual improprieties may have occurred. There was never, however, an allegation of sexual abuse. The daughter never claimed the father did anything at all. An evaluator misinterpreted and determined that based on the child's discomfort with her father that had some sort of sexual quality to it, that the daughter needed to be put into group therapy for victims of sexual abuse. In the process of her therapy, she began to believe that she had been sexually abused by her father. When she was asked what happened, there was simply nothing she could come up with that had anything to do with sexual abuse. After interviewing the father, when he would drop her off at school in the morning, he would say, "Honey, you look really pretty today and pat her on the knee." He remembers doing that once or twice. That pat on the knee got misinterpreted as sexual abuse. But this young girl and her older brother who initially took a protective stance with the father both came to believe that their father was a pedophile. To this day the father has no contact with his children. So, even when there's no specific memory, the subjective memory of what that person was like is easily influenced. It's alarming to know how easy it is to alienate one person from another. Especially children, they are so malleable and open to the process. One can see why using children's testimonies of events that relate to the targeted parent aren't in most cases going to be reliable.

Release of Hostility
As the child participates in the denigration there is an expression of anger. There's an expression of frustration as well that is probably more related to the divorce process, to the disruption of their life, with the legal processes, etc..., and that expression of anger and hostility becomes a release for the child.

The release process becomes a channel or vehicle where all the pent up emotion can then find its way out. Children going through divorce where PAS is not present will act out their emotions. Depending on the child's age, the manifestation of emotions will be different. Toddlers will behave differently than adolescents.

In a typical divorce scenario, one parent leaves the house, "abandons" the family and tries to reestablish themselves in the community, setting-up living quarters, and all that you have to do as you establish another household. In most cases there is some financial hardship even if it is only temporary. Now there are two mortgages or rents to pay, coming from the same income as there was previously. There are other issues such as convenience. The child now has to move from one house to another house. Their free-time is now taken up by visiting one of the parents, the nonresidential parent. They may be separated from their friends. There is a disruption in the children's life that many parents may not realize or don't have the tools to handle. The situation almost naturally creates a target, a displaced target.

Power
The psychodynamics of power, is where venting of rage creates a feeling of power within the child. This is basically another adaptation of a dysfunctional situation. One observation seen many times in the PAS context is the child is empowered. The child, by acting out a particular mission or *campaign of denigration* has been empowered to do so and thereby is charged with taking care of the emotional well-being of the alienating parent. This is communicated to the child by the alienating parent in various ways. For example, the child comes back from visiting the targeted parent, they are enthusiastic, had a good time and then the alienating parent reacts in a very aloof or cool way or even a critical way about the visit.

The alienating parent may even go so far as to suggest that the child should go live with the other parent. This reception very quickly sends a message to not express those feelings in front of them because that is the opposite of taking care of that alienating parent. This reaction is designed to influence the child to do things to make sure to keep the alienating parent happy.

The Energy of Emotion
Living with an alienating parent is continual exposure to emotionally charged situations where the child is in an environment where there are a lot of expressions of anger and hostility directed towards the targeted parent. That negative energy is contagiousness. The child picks up on that energy. Depending on the age of the child, they may look and feel that energy and again feel they are the cause. This is the breeding ground for depression, feelings of rejection, and poor self-esteem in the child, all emanating from the negativity that is in the alienating parent's home. The other side of the coin is when the child visits the targeted parent, there's

another whole energetic field. This energy may not be positive either if the targeted parent is angry or upset about what has happened in their relationship with their child. For the child, school or church may be the only neutral zones.

School or church may not remain neutral however. Individuals in these institutions can get pulled into the dynamics of the parents. During the early stages of PAS with two hostile households, these children will often do fairly well in school. If they are bright and they have had a reasonably good school experience prior to the divorce/separation, they will tend to excel in school. Their academic success is often used as evidence by the alienating parent in court that the child is thriving under their care. So it's not uncommon for these children to do really well in school because the rules there are very clear: study, work hard, do your homework, participate; you get A's. Whereas the rules in the child's personal life, relative to his parents, aren't clear at all.

Gardner uses a metaphor of a tuning fork. When you hit a tuning fork the air takes on the vibration around it and then adjusts its vibration to other objects in its vicinity. An alienating parent's angry vibrations are released to a receptive child. Now the child is vibrating with the aliening parents frequencies and the child carries those vibrations to the targeted parent and communicates that hostility.

One of the things you will see, as children who have been in PAS situations grow up, is a higher incidence of problems in self-esteem. Amy Baker's (2007) work has clearly documented the effects of PAS on adults who were exposed to it during childhood. What has been found is a perception of self that they are not liked by others even when there's no evidence to support their impressions. There is also a tendency to misperceive things because they've been growing up in an environment of misperceptions. Frequently the reality testing of these children will be compromised. Amy Baker (2007) found victims of PAS are candidates for higher incidents of depression. In working with adults, with exposure to PAS, they reveal historical information indicating their parents were divorced when they were children. Quite often, anecdotally, there is a sense of significantly unresolved issues from their own families of origins, that might have happened thirty years earlier, and it was never dealt with and thus never really went away. We are probably going to see these dynamics change, but we can see them now retrospectively. It is a good practice when dealing with adult patients to ask the kind of questions to see if PAS was part of their lives and one may be surprised to find that it is.

Sexual Rivalry
Frequently you will see a divorce situation seem to move smoothly and be uneventful. The process seems smooth as the marital settlement is signed, both parents are cooperating with the visitation arrangements and everything seems to be just fine. Then, all of a sudden, another person is introduced, a significant other, into one of the relationships. Almost on cue, that is when we start to see the PAS activities begin.

The introduction and the timing of PAS are very common because the alienating parent feels threatened. It's not always the case but it's very common. The alienating parent will go out of their way to try to extend the alienation and accelerate it with the co-target, that being the new step-parent. Stepparents are much safer targets because they have no parental rights and children do not have the strong bond initially with the stepparent. This makes it much easier to say negative things about the stepparent that isn't true. There is very little recourse. Frequently, you will see stepparents become targets and then the child's relationship with that stepparent is used as an active way to keep the alienation with the targeted parent going. The alienating behaviors create a tremendous divided loyalty and conflict between the children and the targeted parent when the child is in their physical presence. Complicating things further, the alienating parent gets remarried and the new partner has a rather strong personality. The new partner can become the sparkplug that gets the alienation started, even though they are the new ones in the family. This is a common occurrence.

The environments of children growing up in the context of PAS have psychodynamic characteristics that stress the children. Common to these situations are paranoid, hysterical and narcissistic personality tendencies in the alienating parent. Depending on the personality of the child the impact may be greater on one child versus another in the same family. That is not to say that all alienating parents have these disorders. And not all people with personality disorders are alienating parents. But, there seems to a higher incidence of these features in alienating parents. In the case of a paranoid parent or a parent with paranoid tendencies, they frequently seek wrong doing in others as well as trying to discover what others have it out for them. The children of these parents grow up in an environment where these dynamics are modeled, not challenged and are accelerated and intensified by fear of loss. Recall they already lost one parent through alienation. This situation sort of super charges what would normally happen with a paranoid parent anyway.

Applying Gardner's tuning fork metaphor, the energy of paranoia is being radiated to the child and then you start to see this type of hysterical reaction in the child. In one case we've seen, three children were going to visit the target parent. At the transition site you could observe the children over reacting when they had to go back to the alienating parent. Subsequent testimony, provided by the alienating parent, will talk about the issue of these children screaming at the transition site. In another case where the father lost contact with the child for a brief period, he tried to reestablish the contact by going to the house, the mother refused to let the child talk or see the father. The child was screaming in the background and the father was getting angry, pounding on the door and as this whole scene evolved, the alienated parent was blamed for the whole incident.

It is a relatively frequent occurrence where the angry, frustrated, targeted parent will lose control. The situations they find themselves in border on being almost surreal, a living nightmare, for the targeted parents. The targeted parent's behavior is almost always reported out of context and generalized in the alienating parent's description to the child: "See what I mean, see how abusive he really is".

If we look at some of the earlier work by Harvel Hendrix (1988) in terms of relationship therapy, looking at child's stages of development, we see it in terms of paranoia. Hendrix has a concept of "scared" families which leads to an adult being a clinger or an avoider.

Most of the people that we are seeing now are still children, but Amy Baker's work in retrospective studies shows that PAS does create significant disorders into adulthood. The roadmaps of relationships that are being drawn and these children are being led down the road of psychopathology. The theme really has to do with a displacement of responsibility. We all would agree that taking responsibility is really the theme of mental health, that someone is well adjusted if they can acknowledge their mistakes, learn from them and go forward. Making mistakes can be productive in terms of relationships as well as in terms of self. But these children are being taught that they are not responsible. They are victims, that things have been done to them when in fact, what has been happening is that the often paranoid, narcissistic or hysterical alienating parent is projecting those dysfunctions onto the targeted parent. An interesting aside but seen frequently, the targeted parent will be accused of exactly the things that the alienating parent is doing. Using projection in the strict psychodynamic sense where the alienating parent is unconsciously projecting those malfunctions – and believes them – onto the targeted parent. So you'll see a list of complaints leveled at the targeted parent that are actually being committed by the alienating parent. But when you think about the child growing up in this environment of systematic displacement of responsibility, it only stands to reason that they should have serious problems later in life.

Gardener introduced the idea that some of this could be couched under the DSM-IV of Shared Psychotic Disorder, which is: 297.3 (Folie 'a Deux). This is where a delusion develops in the child who has a close relationship with the alienating parent with an already established delusion. The child's delusion is similar in content, such as the identified faults of the targeted parent that the alienating parent already has.

In one case it was alleged that the father held down a child and beat him with a belt. This supposedly occurred at a particular time and place. When investigated the details of the situation including time and place ruled out the possibility of this being a true description of events. Yet the child and the mother sincerely believed this event occurred. Although they did not take a polygraph examination, we were convinced that if they had, they would have all shown to have been telling the truth!

It is very important to keep in mind that there are many clinical examples. We have been involved in cases where a child has essentially manufactured a story, probably based on something that did happen, however, the perpetrator was not one of the parents. A parent was someone whom that child had not seen in a great many years. While there were some very believable things about the child's claims, there was absolutely nothing in the father's profile that made that at all likely. However, the stepparent who entered the picture had all the characteristics that one would expect to have committed the act. Although it was impossible to prove it is very likely that the incident occurred but not with the targeted parent. In another case a child was being investigated by the Child Protective Team and during the interview, the child identified the perpetrator as his biological father, but at one point in the interview refers to the guilty party as his stepfather. Perhaps an incident substitution, or a "slip of the tongue"? This was never investigated, but the father continues to have supervised visitation.

Chapter 5: Specific PAS Behaviors

These will be behaviors that are typically reported by the targeted parent, by the child sometimes and by other observers.

One relatively common behavior that we have observed in several cases is the destruction of literally every item in the house that belonged to the targeted parent or taking the items and not giving them back. In one extreme case, the kitchen sink and toilets, along with all the other appliances were removed. The targeted parent brought in photographs of the home they shared and absolutely everything was removed except the walls. This included the electric socket covers, all lighting fixtures, everything! Talk about starting from scratch!

Targets for destruction commonly include photographs and any kind of remembrances as if any item left behind that the child could be exposed to would cause some kind of contamination. One of the treatment suggestions that may come up later on is to put some of these things back into place. We've had cases where pictures of the parent were put back into the child's room so that that child could have access to them. In one case a phone was put in the child's room so they could make contact with the other parent.

The attempt to get rid of the pictures, especially when there's been a remarriage, is an attempt to replace the father or mother, whichever it is, with a new spouse or significant other. That's when PAS seems to be much more prevalent as an attempt to just erase any contact or memory of the other parent. On the other hand, if the alienating parent feels extremely victimized by the divorce, they will sometimes leave those mementos around that basically remind themselves and the children about what a terrible person the absent parent was. It's a strange reversal. It is almost like a paradoxical reaction but we've seen that on some occasions. The most common, of course, is getting rid of those objects.

But when they are kept they become sort of a shrine to the abandonment. A broken picture frame, a broken vase or something, imperfectly re-glued as if this was a favorite and it remains as evidence of what he/she did to it!

Destroying the photographs in particular, especially photographs that reflected any kind of positive relationship with the children or the family in general, is common. Also common is destroying any pictures of the extended family, the grandparents. You know, sweep clean and we are going to turn over a new leaf here. This is an expression of the eighth symptom of PAS, which is getting rid of, or the alienation of, the secondary family members.

An important issue here is that, frequently PAS begins when the child learns about the child custody dispute. Can alienating behaviors be executed and observed prior to that point, prior even to divorce and separation? The answer is absolutely yes.

We have read reports and evaluations where evaluators have said "this cannot be PAS because these behaviors were going on before the separation" and that is a terrible misconception of how this works. There was actually a hearing around that particular issue in a case we worked on. The judge had to make a decision whether or not to even entertain the possibility of PAS because the behaviors were reported to have begun prior to the marital separation. While this is more the exception than the rule, it certainly can happen.

This shouldn't be surprising because if a couple is going to divorce, and it is a high conflict situation, whatever the problems that existed in their relationship there are probably going to be vilifications of the other parent in one form or another. When people separate, they always feel that the other person is the unreasonable one and so this gets fed into that sentiment and intensifies.

Frequently we're going to find that the child is permitted to read some of the legal documents that are involved in the case, if they're old enough to read. The legal documentation in a divorce case typically has each of the parties described in excruciating detail in terms of just about every fault known to man. The documents portray each parent's behavior in such language as they appear to be facts. If a child is reading these documentations, then the child is getting indoctrinated in the very arguments that are going to be coming up.

In the divorce process, typically the first thing that happens is the filing of the initial petition. This is the document the petitioner uses to state their strongest case that they have as a reason for the divorce. In other words, if they want to be the primary residential parent, they have to ask for that in the initial petition along with the reason for request. In that petition they have to indicate, in some way, that they are superior to the other parent who is in some way inferior.

The way the legal system works is that you have to state your strongest case at the beginning. Frequently this is the most adversarial and accusatory as well. As humans there is something about information when it is in print. If it is written, it is more believable than the spoken word; therefore, it must be true. So if the child reads these documents, they are going to see very official looking signatures of the parent and attorney, along with all sorts of negative information about the other parent. Obviously no child should ever see any such documents because of their damaging effect. Having said that, however, it is not difficult to leave papers around where the child will make it their business to read the documents. This is one of the more passive, but toxic, ways that the PAS process begins.

A more active way, is where the parent would sit down and literally go over the documents with the child and show them where it says he/she was abusive or here is where he/she had done this or here it states that he/she is an alcoholic and mentions his/her DUI, etc... Because it is in writing, it must be true.

So the whole range of poisoning behaviors of the alienating parent spans from the most subtle to the most obvious with sitting down with legal documents as a very obvious, explicit and direct way to indoctrinate a child. The more passive way is to leave the legal documents around to be found. Unfortunately, both tactics are commonly done.

Another common behavior is where the alienating parent regretfully tells the child that he can no longer go to their favorite restaurant, McDonald's, Burger King or wherever, because they are not getting enough child support.

It is at this point that the child is incorporated into the process when he or she learns about child support. Again, stating the obvious, the child should not know about that; should not know about the amounts or any of the terms of that process. But when it comes up in a way that the child is being deprived because of the behavior of the other parent, such as we don't have enough money because of your father or mother, it begins to build a bias against that parent. This coupled with other indoctrinating information and the child's mind begins to be set. We are not able to do things because of them. This tactic of course vilifies the other parent and victimizes the parent and child as well, causing them to be more bonded in opposition to the targeted parent.

Sometimes it might even occur to the child to steal money. We have seen cases where a child was actually stealing money from a sibling who was living with the other parent and got away with it for quite a while. They were actually stealing money along with all kinds of other things. One will often find things disappear and then turn up at the other parent's household with the child doing so under the instructions of the alienating parent.

Professionals working with children in high conflict divorces should insure that the children do not get into the issue of money; they need to be sheltered from that topic. There is no reason to share financial matters with children. Doing so will only engender feelings of insecurity that are unnecessary. Avoiding money issues with children is generally a good idea regardless if the other parent is the cause. Children do not need to feel any more insecure about their life situation beyond what the divorce is already causing.

We are not suggesting that a parent or therapist falsely tell a child that "everything is O.K." After all, the child's world has changed dramatically. Their parents are no longer together. They are living now with one, traveling between houses to see the other parent. Their life is totally upside down and now a parent or therapist is telling them, "Everything is OK". Yet they have a lot of things that are to the contrary as indicators suggesting the situation is not "OK."

Another common behavior found in the PAS situation is where the alienating parent exaggerates the other parent's minor psychological problems. Here is where the computer metaphor comes back in to play. We are all humans and every one of us has an unconscious (operating system). Every one of us has imperfections, faults, something that is not OK about us; hence being human. Divorces are incredibly stress inducing and we know that when a human is placed under stressful conditions they will display their faults and at times in an exaggerated way.
 While we all make mistakes, an alienating parent will frequently exaggerate the other parent's faults and lifestyle. For example, one beer does not an alcoholic make. But it will not be uncommon to hear, during a custody evaluation, a parent expressing concern about the other parent's alcoholism, only to discover that they either don't drink or drink very little.

The child is frequently interrogated upon returning from a visit with such dialog as "at daddy's you saw he had a beer, didn't you?" This is followed with an affirmation like "See? What did I tell you? I told you he has a drinking problem".

This questioning and dialog makes the child vigilant about the target parent's behavior and will cause the child to come back and report. Of course this leads to more questions about areas where there are no problems at all.

This is an interesting example of a dynamic because the child from this point on is on a mission to report back things in some way. They may begin to exaggerate things on their own. So then the child goes back and reports on the targeted parent. The alienating parent in all likelihood takes the child's statements to be truthful and then becomes more alarmed. In the process the child is reinforced for his or her contribution to the alienation. One can see this process where the child begins to embellish upon reality by making it worse than it really was because he or she gets rewarded for the reporting to the alienating parent. One can also see the alienating parent really begins to solidify their beliefs which before they were only suspicious about. This new evidence fuels their reason to be critical of the targeted parent. So one can see in this example how the shared delusional system can actually begin and ultimately progress into a full blown delusion or false belief about the targeted parent. This becomes fertile ground for the false beliefs to become a common or shared knowledge between an alienating parent and child. While there may be other aspects of this dynamic situation, at least one can see how this mechanism as described here can operate.

In one case we recall there was a father who had a history of being treated for depression. It turns out he was a physician who never missed a day of work and was a very high functioning person but he had been treated for depression at an earlier time in his life, not unlike many people in our culture. His depression was used and labeled as mental illness, which appeared in the pleadings, it appeared in all kinds of things and the children knew. As the children got older, they would make reference to their father's "mental illness" in their conversations. This is just an example of how terrific these situations get and how people's "faults" get exaggerated. In particular this is an example of how the fault finding is encouraged by the alienating parent.

A word of caution, however, is in order. Things are generally not what they appear to be. We are making the case for a thorough investigation by the professionals in these cases. For example, a case was recently referred which an attorney suggested there was alienation going on it needed to stop. The case involved the children returning from their visits with their father and telling their mother that the father was mean to them. The children were becoming reluctant to see the father. When the mother would confront the father an argument would ensue and communication would be terminated. On the next visit, the father would talk to the children about "telling on him" to their mother. In the absence of good communication skills this creates a vicious cycle of who is telling what to whom. And, as one would expect the father was alleging alienation by the mother. Upon investigation, however, what the children tried to explain to the father was that they felt he was demeaning them because of the manner in which he would speak to them. Interestingly, even during a counseling session with the father and children, he spoke in a very gruff and direct manner, which the children responded to with tears. When confronted by the counselor about his style of communication to the children, he insisted they needed feedback and needed to learn to take criticism. Needless to say, he didn't take the counselor's observations too well. The point is that what may appear to be alienation on the surface is a different story when peeling back the layers. This was an excellent case of a dysfunctional family. The alleged target was contributing to the children's rejection and the mother frankly was somewhat passive in encouraging the children to visit.

A common question or statement encountered in this work is the notion that the "children need to know the truth." A good rule of thumb or counter to this argument is to first answer the question, "what specific benefit will be child derive from knowing this new information?" So, examples are: a parent was once treated for depression, a parent had a DUI, a parent had a homosexual relationship once in their life, one parent was expelled from school, a parent was sexually abused as a child, etc. It is certainly in the realm of possibility that one could come up with a justification that might give some rationale reason to reveal this information to a child. However, for the most part, a child does not need to know information, such as above, about their parents. A more interesting question, from a child custody investigation point of view, is "what is the motivation for a parent to reveal this information"? In other words, given that this information was previous known, why reveal it now? What would possess someone to share this information? The argument routinely is "the child has to know the truth." Our question is "why"? How will they benefit?

The child's participation in sharing and exaggerating a parent's faults is a reinforcing issue for an alienating parent. We think that is really an important thing to pause on. That is, once the child is shuttling back and forth and they realize that there's some reward in "telling" for them. There is some emotional reward for coming back and reporting some misstep or some mistake or something that the alienating parent would be upset about. As they do this they are drawn closer to the alienating parent. They'll be hugged and they'll be treated in a protective way; rewarded. Then as they bring back that information, that may be exaggerated, on their own, without anybody else's help, and the alienating parent begins to believe it, the whole situation snowballs. It gets bigger and bigger as it goes along over time. We really think that is one of the mechanisms that these things get to be built upon. It becomes a self-reinforcing cycle between the alienating parent and the child.

Early in the divorce process parents do not trust each other very well. This is a time when parents might not behave all that well, either, but they are not trying to alienate the children from one another; there is no PA or PAS. When a parent is doing something they shouldn't do and it is brought to their attention, it is noteworthy that the parent will listen, think about their behavior and possibly acknowledge it. Frequently they will modify their behavior. An alienating parent won't. They will look at you like you have "two-heads" and say, "Oh, I never did that". "I don't know what you're talking about". Or "it's fine, it's not a problem".

There is a big difference when there is that acknowledgement, that responsibility, and the desire to do what is best for the child. It is really a diagnostic hallmark.

Another diagnostic hallmark is requiring the visiting parent to park in front of the house or away from the house and blow the horn so that they don't have to go near the house to retrieve the child for visitation. This is almost stereotypic behavior of the alienating parent. Does every case where this is happening have PA and PAS going on? Obviously not but it's almost in every PA and PAS case. We have had one parent state that they were forced to park across the street and retrieve the children. At first blush it seemed like a PAS situation. Upon closer examination there was an injunction against that parent from going near the house and the other parent. The injunction was a legitimate legally imposed restriction.

When requiring a visiting parent to remain distant from the children's home and there is no legal reason to do so, it sends a message to the child that says there is something dangerous about that person. There is something terribly wrong with them that they can't even get on the property. There's something really bad and if the alienating parent is reluctant for the child to go on that visitation, it even makes that parent seem protective. So this tactic helps to further enmesh the relationship between the child and that alienating parent. As these behaviors continue the PAS process progresses along.

Another behavior that is frequently engaged in is when the alienating parent is spending time with each child alone engaged in bedtime prayers. They ask God to bless a long list of friends and relatives, of course leaving the other parent off the list. In custody evaluations the evaluator hears this all the time, especially when the child is asked questions about their bedtime routine.   If you ask the right questions about things such as that, you will often hear that said very explicitly.

We had an interesting case where a mom was a stay at home mom. She would put the children to sleep at night and leave the children with the father so she could go food shopping. Every time she would quickly walk out the back door, except this one time. She hesitated before she exited the house. She then heard the father go to the children's room, wake the children up to tell them that mommy is going out drinking, over her friend's house, not to worry. Can you imagine the actual shock that mother had when she heard that message that these children were getting? From then on she would be able to hear this every time she went to the store at night. He wouldn't go with her to the store because it was too late and the children were in bed.

These are classic examples of how this occurs and that happens while these people were still together. Even though there was no separation one can see how the seeds were being planted.

A common alienating maneuver is to insist that the targeted parent not attend any school recitals, sports events; simply stay away. If they do attend, then they are required to sit some distance from the other parent, friends, relatives and siblings. If they violate that request and they sit close to them, the alienating parent causes a public scene and sometimes even gets the police involved. This is a very common one that you will see repeatedly. Sometimes you will see notes that a parent can produce that say "Do not sit near us because the children don't want to be with you, they're embarrassed to have you at their game". Those notes, by the way, in a litigation sense can be very helpful to demonstrate a parent's alienating behavior.

The alienating parent sometimes will use a neutrality maneuver claiming to be in the middle. This is the way the alienating parent tries to stay out of the main battle and appears to be innocent. They don't want to make any apparent decisions, and try to appear neutral. The children are resisting the visitation with the targeted parent but the alienating parent refrains from encouraging that relationship. They commonly just say "I'm not going to force them to go, it's up to them". We have one father who stated that "the son can call his mother any time he wants to, I'm just not going to force him to do it; it's up to him; I'm not preventing him from calling."

Whenever you hear "it's up to them", what that is really saying is that the child has to make the choice. If the child is in a setting where it is clearly known that that parent does not want the children to be with the other parent, the children are given the choice. The children are put in the middle and in a position to have to resist the pressure from both sides. This then becomes feedback to that alienating parent that reinforces their thinking and you can see how the delusion can begin and sustain itself. They may start out saying, "I don't want them to go over there so   I'm not going to force them." The child then resists going and then the parent begins to think, well, there really is something wrong. They really don't want to go. And you can see again this logic feeding upon itself, like a snowball getting bigger and bigger as it goes down a hill.

It is important for everyone to recognize that it is the healthy parent that is going to encourage the relationship with the other parent. This fact seems to be recognized in Florida law.

In fact, Florida Statute 61.13 provides guidelines for making timesharing decisions. The relevant factors are:

(a) The demonstrated capacity and disposition of each parent to facilitate and encourage a close and continuing parent-child relationship, to honor the time-sharing schedule, and to be reasonable when changes are required.

(l) The demonstrated capacity of each parent to communicate with and keep the other parent informed of issues and activities regarding the minor child, and the willingness of each parent to adopt a unified front on all major issues when dealing with the child.

So the courts have recognized that the best interests of children are service by a parent who will encourage a relationship with both parents. We think this is a very important point. The best way to protect children from the effects of divorce psychologically is to minimize the loss. That is, have access to both parents without penalty. And so, therefore, if the child has a problem or complains about the other parent, instead of jumping on that critical perspective and supporting it, the proper thing to do is to try to almost apologize for that parent and to explain in understanding terms what really is best for that child. Part of what is best is for a child to have is a good relationship with both parents. The healthy parent will understand that immediately while an alienating parent will look at you like you have two-heads. In some cases they simply don't get it. They truly believe that they are the best and only parent the child needs.

In an interview situation, you are dealing with one of the parents and they preface their statements to you with "believe me or let me be frank, I really want the children to have a good relationship with the other parent." This prepared statement may cause some flags to go up. More often than not, in conversations between people we do not have to preface our statements with "believe me, I'm telling you truth, let me be honest with you, can I be frank?" Why? Generally we are not trying to convince someone we are about to tell the truth, it's assumed most of the time. When someone prefaces their statements this way what they are really saying is, "unless I preface this in this way I must not otherwise be telling the truth."

Another alienating behavior is where the alienating parent threatens the child. If you don't stop doing that, then I'm going to send you to go live with the other parent. What that does is denigrate the value of that other parent in the child's eyes by implying that the home of the targeted parent is a place of punishment. Not only that, it exacerbates fears of abandonment. The child's already been taught that the parent who they're not with has abandoned them, so now they are being faced with two terrible things. One they could be abandoned by the other parent and then have to go live with the inferior parent as a punishment. It is amazing that PA and PAS are not explicitly cited as a form of child abuse and neglect, although we believe it meets the definition of abuse as presented in FL Chapter 39.

Alienating behaviors also come in the form of intimidation. One alienating parent will tell the child, "I can see why you hate him but you'll have to go and visit or else the judge will get mad at me". This sends the message that it is the child's responsibility to fix and to protect the alienating parent. It also reinforces the evil of the other parent. It has all those messages woven into it.

Purposely sending children to the other parent's house with inappropriate clothing is another alienating tactic. This happens so much. Mismatched clothing, wrong sizes, forgetting really vital items, bathing suits, etc... just essentially sabotages the visit. This makes it not fun for the child at the other parent's place because they don't have all the things they need to have whatever the fun was going to be.

We have seen this a lot, the alienating parent does not inform the other parent about hospitalizations, serious sicknesses or illnesses. The child is told that the other parent didn't come to visit them as some kind of proof that they lack concern for them. Even if the child isn't told that, the child is in the hospital without a visit from the other parent, thereby sending a message without saying a word. That is, in this time of crisis, with hospitals being a scary place for children, the other parent wasn't there and therefore, wasn't able to provide support throughout the traumatic experience. Additionally, upon the child's discharge from the hospital, the parent makes no comment about their hospitalization because they didn't know anything about it. This sends a further message to the child that the parent doesn't really care. It disengages them; it makes that parent more peripheral to the child's life. This, by the way, is the consequence of many of these maneuvers that exclude the other parent from the child. It creates a situation which makes that parent less aware of all the details in that child's life and detail is the primary ingredient of intimacy.

We have alienating parents that decompress a child's enthusiasm about their recent visit and the events that happened during that visit with the targeted parent. They are basically saying, "Look, I don't want to really hear it. That's between you and them". The result is a sort of blocking that has its effect of taking away some of the pleasure of that experience. Ultimately this will actually affect the bond between the child and the targeted parent.

This negative reaction or shutting down of the communication from the child regarding their visit sends a very clear message to the child. Again, as with other alienating tactics, the theme or fuel of this disorder is fear; specifically fear of loss. It sends the message that "I don't want you to have a good time over there. That displeases me. You're with me most of the time and you don't want to displease me." So typically you will find that the children will come back from a visitation enthusiastic about their seeing the other parent about once or twice and then with repeated exposure to this negativity their enthusiasm will disappear. Very quickly they learn what to say and what not to say and how to present what they did during the visit. Typically, what they present will be a very pale or even a negative picture of what they did. All of this feeds the alienating parent's growing belief in the maladaptive nature of the targeted parent. While at the same time this feeds into a delusional cycle where the child begins taking whatever was an ideal, a positive, and making it worse to please the alienating parent (out of fear), which then causes the alienating parent to even feel worse about the targeted parent. As a consequence, reality gets stretched out of shape in a much disfigured way, to the point of it becoming a delusion.

Another instance is the parent who has the right of first refusal for visitation. That is, for whatever reason the alienating parent can't be with the child for an evening. Even though they are supposed to ask the targeted parent to watch the child they find another person to be with the child. They bring in other people; they'll go out of their way to place the child with anyone other than the other parent. We had a case where they actually put the child in daycare for a mom's night out in order to prevent the other parent from having the child and insisted that that parent pay for it! When the targeted parent protests, they are then accused of being too smothering of the child; simply amazing.

This section described some of the common behaviors of an alienating parent. There are certainly others but the reader can see that there is a consistent theme that is repeated over and over and the more one works with these families, the more you will begin to see these common tactics repeated.

Chapter 6: The Counseling and Evaluation Settings

We want to discuss some of the things that may be beneficial to a mental health professional either working as a therapist or as an evaluator.

Quite often members of a divorcing family will have already been to a mental health professional and frequently there is or was a whole group of counselors or clinicians that have been involved in a case. Frequently a clinician will find that if the case has matured for a while, the targeted parent will have gone to some therapist, frequently arranged by the alienating parent. The target parent will describe negative feeling about that particular meeting. This is very common. As with schools and doctors, a therapist may have been influenced or biased against the targeted parent; it does happen. With all the ethical standards and best practices aside, bias among professional counselors and therapists does happen. In a sense they become programmed to be suspicious of this particular, targeted parent.

One possible rule of thumb relative to a case when there is PAS is that there really should only be one therapist. This may fly in the face of a lot of the standard opinions, that everybody should have their own therapist, every child and every parent. In the case of when PAS is afoot, multi professionals treating the individuals in a family can be a dangerous thing. It can create divisiveness where each therapist begins to champion the person they are seeing, with a suspiciousness of all the others. It is very uncommon when that doesn't happen.

If a therapist starts to suspect PAS without verbally planting that seed with the client, it would be beneficial to try to identify the symptoms that are going on in the case. See if there is evidence, documentation, testimony, etc... on some of the behaviors and symptoms. Try to put together a picture that seems to be consistent with what we've talked about. Understand that no one is perfect. Everybody is going to come in with baggage (their operating system), if you will. And they are going to open their files and you need to look at them with a somewhat more objective eye to say that maybe, PAS just might be a possibility in this case. One of the things we are trying to stress here is that in working with adults and children in a divorce situation, it is very important to be open to the possibilities. A serious concern is when a professional negates the possibility of PAS because they don't believe it's a syndrome. If one does not believe in something, they cannot find it. If one of the parents becomes educated in PAS and the symptoms, they may come in to the therapist or evaluator trying to explain why they see it as PAS. The professional who doesn't see the family situation as a potential PAS scenario may dismiss the discussion and dismiss the targeted parent; ultimately missing the situation entirely. All we are asking is to have this possibility in mind; to think if this could be going on, especially if a child is making complaints about a parent. It is very important to ask questions about the validity of the complaints.

Well the opposite may also be true. Not every case walking through the door is a PAS case. Just because a child has an issue with a parent doesn't mean that there is a parent who is an alienator. So the cases are really asking for objectivity, in the sense of looking at the details of a case. One suggestion is the idea of looking at developing a custody evaluation and developing collateral interviews. Now, if you are a therapist in a case you can't be the evaluator. If you are a targeted parent you can suggest to your attorney that a custody evaluation be ordered by the court.

It is our feeling that therapists and counselor need to be more directive as opposed to passive in the sense of having an unconditional positive regard for the client. Many therapists are trained to have this orientation. We are not making a case to be obnoxious, aggressive and hurtful. But we are making a case to be more direct. That is, telling their client what to do and what not to do in some of these cases, because they need to know what can hurt them and what is beneficial. For example, parents need to be encouraged to allow their children to be with the other parent. Parents need to be told not to say inappropriate things to their children. It is not helpful to the parent or the children to interfere with visits with the other parent.

It is important to realize that targeted parents are walking around in a state of shock. They're walking around depressed. They are victimized, whether that's part of their personality or not, is to be determined, but they may be being victimized in this particular situation and they might need some very clear direction, guidelines in terms of what is appropriate and what's inappropriate as mentioned earlier. And some therapists and attorneys may not be comfortable with that role. They don't see themselves as having to do that. If you're the therapist for this person and you're working with them, then perhaps it is more like a coaching relationship then it is in terms of a psychotherapeutic one.

This holds true with the alienating parent as well, but in a different way. It is important to help them to be able to identify those things that they are doing or not doing relative to the other parent. Also, alienating parents may not be aware that what they are doing is damaging to the children. The behaviors and tactics discussed earlier ultimately harm the children. A parent who thinks that what they are doing is simply hurting the other parent needs to know otherwise.

Parents should be able to come in and to ask a therapist directly if they are aware that PAS might be going on. Ask the therapist how familiar they are with PAS. How many PAS cases have they had in the past? Are they comfortable working in this area? This can be a difficult area for a therapist to work in. More likely than not, they are going to be called in to give testimony. How comfortable are they going to court? And more likely than not, they are going to have records scrutinized and they will probably be deposed and questioned about their judgment. So it is important for a therapist to go into a case fully aware and being able to respond to those challenges.

A word of caution: If a therapist is not familiar with PAS and they are treating the case in whatever capacity, as an individual's therapist or a family therapist, and the children are in some stage of the alienation process there is a danger that the therapist will actually be counterproductive. They may end up treating a parent as though they have been an abusive parent, which is a disservice to them and it plays into the alienation. This is a very common. In other words, a child will come in or a therapist may be even ordered by a court to do reunification therapy between a child and the targeted parent. More often than not, however, the court will not identify the source of the alienation. The court will simply request the therapist to rehabilitate the relationship; simply fix it. Frequently a therapist will not want to know the background information and will essentially wait for the child to be "ready" to see the parent before they encourage more contact. That's essentially the same kind of treatment children have when they have been abused by a parent. They are not pushed too much. The child's feelings are taken very seriously and at face value.

However, in a PAS case, if the therapy is conducted in this manner, that will actually serve to support the alienation. In other words, in a PAS case, the child has to be coached to have more contact between them and the targeted parent, sometimes over the protests of the child. So if the therapist is unaware of that, they will fall into the old standard approach which will actually not be neutral. It will be ultimately injurious to the child because therapy becomes a place where the alienation is acted out and documented. The therapist then becomes a voice to testify on behalf of and in support of the alienation, frequently without even realizing it. Unfortunately this is a common occurrence.

-94-

What appears to apply to therapists is also related to attorneys. Parents need to seek out attorneys who have some familiarity with PAS, or who are at least are aware of it. They may not understand the whole syndrome piece to it, but at least they are aware of PAS as a possible issue. They need to understand some of the controversies, which we will cover in the next chapter.

Attorneys need to be aware of the controversies that are typically levied against the concept of PAS and they need to be comfortable with defending against them. They ought to have experts that they are comfortable working with like therapists who are experienced and knowledgeable in dealing with PA and PAS. This way, they really are coming into the case to work with the targeted parent and are trying to minimize the destruction of the alienation process. They need to be looking toward the reunification if that has been an issue in that case.

The passage of time in these cases is not a neutral factor. The longer a case takes the more alienation occurs. Time is significant. As a clinician, if you're hearing the details of a case and you ask what their lawyer said to do about a particular situation, and the response is, "Nothing! He said it would just go away", you may want to try talking to that attorney and help them understand PA and PAS better.

We've included this chapter because if you work with these families going through PA and PAS, you will become aware of these issues. If you're a therapist, clinician, or an evaluator working in these cases and working with lawyers, you may be working with a lawyer who doesn't understand the limitations of your role. The most common example of that would be an attorney saying, "I've got this case. I'm pretty sure it's an alienation case and I'd like you to review the documents, talk to one parent (because you can't talk to the other one as they will refuse), read over the case documentation and I want you to write a report saying that this is PAS". A therapist, counselor, psychologist cannot, under any circumstances, do that. To do so would be a major ethical violation.

A lawyer may not be fully aware of that because their focus is primarily on what they can do for their client and they are looking for a way to make their case. Most lawyers and judges do not understand the ethical standards under which psychologists and mental health professionals operate.

Because they don't understand, they will ask a therapist to do things that they just shouldn't do. We can't tell you how many times we've seen a marriage and family therapist do a "custody evaluation" based on a single interview of one parent and maybe the child but never saw the other parent. Custody evaluation is in quotes because technically it can't be one unless it is conducted properly. It's difficult to believe, but that does go on.

Chapter 7: Current Controversies Regarding PAS

PAS continues to elicit controversy in both the mental health and legal arenas.   Interestingly, the growing body of literature, both theoretical and empirical research, fails to quiet this debate.   This chapter will briefly summarize the issues at hand.   The controversies appear to center around whether PAS is a reliable and valid diagnosis and thereby properly admissible in divorce/custody cases.   Other issues include the appropriate treatment modalities, the appropriateness of the term "syndrome" and last, and probably least, the issue that PAS is not presently in the American Psychiatric Association's Diagnostic and Statistical Manual – Fourth Edition (DSM-IV).

Dr. Richard A. Warshak (2001) published an excellent article entitled: *Current Controversies Regarding Parental Alienation Syndrome* in the American Journal of Forensic Psychology, in 2001.   He presented very objective and comprehensive arguments focusing on the issues commonly cited against PAS.   Some of this work will be briefly summarized here.   He stated that the detractors of PAS often argue that:

1. PAS oversimplifies the etiology of children's alienation
2. Children's alienation from one parent is normal, therefore, not a disorder at all
3. PAS leads to confusion in clinical work with children, it's not reliable or valid
4. PAS lacks a scientific foundation to be considered a syndrome
5. PAS as a diagnosis, its course and treatment are inadmissible
6. PAS is anti-feminist and unfairly blames women
7. PAS forces children to be with a hated parent who is possibly an abuser
8. PAS is not in the DSM-IV therefore, it doesn't exist

1. PAS oversimplifies the etiology of children's alienation

Dr. Warshak (2001) points out that part of the problem with this issue is that many who claim to doubt the authenticity of PAS fail to comprehend all of the elements that go into the syndrome. In order for PAS to be a valid diagnosis, there has to be three elements present:

1. there has to be a *campaign of denigration* on the part of the child
2. there has to be little or no valid rationale for the campaign
3. the child's alienation has to be the result of the work of an alienating parent or adult in the child's life

Many detractors of PAS fail to consider 2 and 3, but focus instead on the denigration by the child of the targeted parent. If there are valid reasons for a child to reject a parent, then the denigration is not the result of programming by an alienating parent, and then there is no PAS. To pursue a PAS diagnosis under these conditions would be a misuse of the terminology.

A number of health care professionals working in the divorce arena have used reported phenomenon analogous to Gardner's term "PAS". Wilhelm Reich in 1949, for example, referred to alienating parents as seeking "revenge on the parent through robbing him or her of the pleasure of the child". Wallerstein and Kelly, out spoken critics of PAS, and Dr. Richard Gardner, in 1980, described children who "were particularly vulnerable to being swept up into the anger of one parent against the other... They were faithful...in efforts to hurt the other parent. Not infrequently, they turned on the parent they had loved and had been very close to prior to the marital separation" (p.77). In 1989, Wallerstein coined the term "Medea Syndrome", referring to parents who facilitate the alienation of a child from an ex-spouse. These children are "overburdened" because they must attend to the needs of a disturbed parent.

Critics are frequently seen to describe essentially the same phenomenon but are using their own terminology.

2. Children's alienation from one parent is normal, therefore, not a disorder at all

It is possible that some children's relationships with one parent or even both parents may become estranged temporarily in divorce situations. But to consider parent alienation by a child as normal seems to be contradictory of what we know about child development, research on children from divorced families, parent-child relationships or even human relations for that matter. Conflicts in families, divorced or otherwise, can cause harm to children. It certainly matters how the conflicts are played out. The amount or degree of harm to children correlates with the severity of the conflicts. Relatively minor conflicts cause relatively minor effects; physical violence causes more emotional and psychological damage to the children. It is almost universal for children of divorce to want and wish that their parents get back together. It is also very common that children blame themselves for the divorce. Throughout the range of discord in a family, however, children want to be with both parents and it is departures from this sentiment that are abnormal, not the other way around. So to be perfectly clear, it is abnormal for a child to hate their parent without a valid reason.

3. PAS leads to confusion in clinical work with children because PAS is not reliable or valid

Kelly and Johnson in 2001 thought PAS oversimplified the causes of alienation and that it leads to confusion and misuse in litigation. In order to rectify PAS' shortcoming they proposed "the alienated child". According to them, the alienated child "expresses, <u>freely</u> and <u>persistently</u>, <u>unreasonable</u> negative feelings and beliefs toward a parent that are <u>significantly disproportionate</u> to the child's actual experience with that parent" (underline for emphasis). Warshak points out that this concept retains two of the three essential elements in PAS. These include: the free and persistent expression of negative feelings which corresponds to the *campaign of denigration*. The second one includes the unreasonable negative feelings that correspond to the unjustified aspect to the child's complaints. They explicitly remove the "programming" parent and place the primary focus on the child's observable behavior. Only after a therapist documents the child's behavior do they then assess why the child is now rejecting a parent. Presumably if a therapist discovers a parent has been indoctrinating a child, then all the elements of PAS would be accounted for. All three of the PAS elements are there, their order, however, varies. It is somewhat unclear why Kelly and Johnson's (2001) proposed investigation is less confusing than Gardner's concept of PAS, when in fact, by their own words are apparently similar.

Reliability

The term reliability refers to the degree to which a measure or diagnosis, is consistent on repeated trials or among different observers. PAS has high reliability if different clinicians, examining the same children reach agreement on whether or not a child has the syndrome. It is not necessary for clinicians to reach one hundred percent agreement in order to qualify as having reached a scientifically acceptable level of reliability. This rarely happens now with currently acceptable or non-controversial diagnoses. Doctors often disagree on a diagnosis, hence the need for a second opinion.

The description of PAS symptoms and the description of the behaviors seen in the alienated child as presented earlier appear to be apparently clear. In fact, several recent studies have demonstrated the reliability of identifying the symptoms of PAS. Janelle Burrill in 2001 corroborated the observations and definitions of PAS as well as the levels of severity as described by Gardner. Carlos Rueda in 2004 demonstrated a significant level of concordance among raters of PAS cases, thereby demonstrating the reliability of the levels of severity.

The argument that PAS is not a reliable concept appears to be quickly fading away.

On an anecdotal level we see commonality among researchers. Gardner (1998), for example, cites one of the symptoms of PAS as "weak, absurd or frivolous rationalizations for the deprecation". Kelly and Johnson (2001) cite "trivial or false reasons used to justify hatred" in an alienated child. While Kelly and Johnson (2001) are explicit detractors of PAS it is noteworthy the similarity of the symptom's descriptions they offer in lieu of Gardner's presentation.

Validity
The issues of validity address the question as to whether PAS accurately describes a disturbance suffered by some children. To establish the validity of PAS, the scientific literature must demonstrate that the clinical observations of the symptoms are representative of a certain population of children; those who are alienated from a targeted parent as a result of an alienating parent's behavior and with contributions by the child. Dr. Warshak (2001) tells us that there are generally two stages in the validity process. First, other clinicians report on their experiences related to the issue at hand. Second, empirical research is conducted with larger samples sizes using standardized measures and appropriate controls to test hypotheses. We are now witnessing the second stage of this process.

PAS is emerging in the clinical literature virtually on a daily basis. Divorcing parents, attorneys and mental health professionals are ever increasingly becoming aware of the problem. There is now an organized volume of literature, including articles and research that address the appropriate identification and treatment of children suffering with this problem. The frequency of these reports and their similarity to Gardner's descriptions clearly lends support to the validity of PAS. As Warshak (2001) stated "the burgeoning literature is evidence of the utility of the PAS concept". We will not go into an in depth presentation of the research in supporting the validity, but will refer readers to Warshark's, Gardner's and other's works. The reader is referred to the *International Handbook of Parental Alienation Syndrome*, edited by Gardner, Sauber and Lorandos (2006). A study worth mentioning at this stage is the work published by the American Bar Association (ABA) entitled *Children Held Hostage* (Clawar & Rivlin, 1991). This was a 12-year study of 700 divorced families, which demonstrated the extent divorced or divorcing parents program their children against the other parent. The ABA study provided empirical support for the validity of PAS with significant descriptive data on how children are intentionally brainwashed or alienated from one parent by the other parent. Systematic empirical research is beginning to come in to validate the cluster of symptoms that characterizes PAS. Last, but certainly not least, the book *Parental Alienation DSM-5 and ICD-11*, edited by William Bernet, M.D. (2010) lists contributions by 70 professionals with references from 30 countries on six continents. This book alone is somewhat of a testament of the validity of PAS.

4. PAS lacks a scientific foundation to be considered a syndrome

It is far too common to hear professionals routinely dismiss PAS as a syndrome. A syndrome is a grouping of signs and symptoms based on their frequent co-occurrence that may suggest a common underlying pathogenesis, course, familial pattern, or treatment selection. PAS as many others have come to discuss it clearly meets this definition.

As Dr. Warshak (2001) has pointed out some have argued that PAS does not qualify as a syndrome because not every child who is exposed to an alienating parent develops the same disorder. In medicine, including psychiatry, the same pathological agent can produce different outcomes in different individuals. This generally does not invalidate the disorder or the disease. For example, victims of rape do not always develop a post-traumatic stress disorder (PTSD), which by the way was originally termed a syndrome, and was not immediately accepted into the medical/psychological community. The fact that some victims experience traumas without developing PTSD does not negate or disqualify PTSD as a diagnosis. We will revisit the analogy of PTSD later when we talk about the DSM-IV. There are other examples of diagnoses that do not manifest themselves identically in every person who is exposed to the preconditions of the disorder. So to argue this point in this manner is of little value.

The designation "syndrome" conveys legitimacy that some may believe requires more rigorous empirical research. Opponents of PAS believe that using the term "syndrome" in court may strengthen judicial confidence in the concept thereby enhancing its testimonial value and reliability.

A presumptive concern about the use of syndrome evidence is that expert witnesses may offer a collection of symptoms as proof that there is one cause, even in the absence of verification of the proposed cause. In PAS cases this would mean after determining a child had the symptoms of an alienated child the expert would presume the existence of an alienating parent as causing the alienating child's behavior. This is clearly a misuse of PAS. The manipulations of the alienating parent must be clearly identified in order to diagnose PAS.

PAS testimony should not be used as a test of whether the aligned parent was instrumental in the child's alienation. But expert testimony can provide a court with alternative explanations for a child's negative or fearful behavior. PAS testimony can assist a court in assessing children's social, psychological and memory functions. If PAS is misdiagnosed, as with children who have not been alienated, or there is justification for rejecting a parent based on the parent's behavior, expert testimony on PAS may help a court in sorting these particulars out.

As Dr. Warshak stated in his 2001 paper:

"Testimony by an expert knowledgeable about the strategies that parents use to promulgate and support alienation, the extent to which children can be manipulated to reject and denigrate a parent, the extent to which children are suggestible, the mechanics of stereotype induction, and the psychological damage associated with involving children in parental hostilities, may assist the court in determining the proper amount of weight to give a child's explicitly stated preferences and statements regarding each parent. The expert can demonstrate that a child's statement of preference, even when executed in an affidavit, does not necessarily reflect the history of that child's relationship with the non-preferred parent, particularly when the child totally rejects the non-preferred parent".

To deny a court such a benefit because of the fear of the terminology "syndrome" is to literally deny justice in a family law case. It simply makes no sense.

5. PAS as a diagnosis, its course and treatment are inadmissible

The U.S. Supreme Court decision in, *Daubert v. Merrell Dow Pharmaceuticals, Inc.* (1993), provided a **non-exclusive** criteria.   The application of the *Daubert* decision to expert testimony relative to mental health issues is very much up for debate.   For some, the *Daubert* decision ends psychological and psychiatric testimony because these fields are so subjective in nature and cannot meet the *Daubert* criteria. Others see little impact of *Daubert* on psychological testimony in criminal cases, including the admissibility of battered women syndrome evidence. In child custody cases, however, it is not clear whether courts are using *Daubert* criteria to evaluate expert testimony on the best interests of children issue. The *Dauber criteria are:*

> 1) Is the theory or technique at issue testable, and has it been tested?

2) Has the theory or technique been subjected to peer review and publication?
3) In the case of scientific techniques, what is the known or potential error rate and are there standards controlling the technique's operation?
4) Does the technique enjoy general acceptance within the scientific community?

The literature is now catching up on these criteria with PAS being tested much more frequently and comprehensively than ever before. There is an ever increasing library of peer review publications. As reported earlier the error rate of diagnosis and inter-rater reliability is being examined and reported.

There is significant difficulty in applying the *Daubert* decision as it applies its criteria of scientific admissibility to clinical testimony. General acceptance of the clinical evidence in the relevant scientific community is one of the *Daubert* factors. This criterion is a carry-over from the previously accepted standard rendered in *Frye v. United States* (1923) for scientific testimony. Many courts, however, exempt psychological syndrome testimony from a *Frye* analysis. PAS as a diagnosis is widely recognized among mental health professionals, albeit controversial, therefore, the criterion "that a sizeable group of professionals find plausible, based on their specialized knowledge" appears satisfied. It already has, in fact, in Hillsborough County FL *Kilgore v. Boyd* (2000). The 13th Circuit Court of Hillsborough County, FL, ruled that, "PAS had gained enough acceptance in the scientific community to satisfy the Frye test criteria for admissibility". PAS has been recognized in 30 countries on six continents (Bernet, 2010).

Another index of the general acceptance of PAS is the growing professional literature on PAS in peer-review journals. Also, the American Psychological Association, in its *Guidelines for Child Custody Evaluations in Divorce Proceedings* (1994) includes Gardner's works on this subject in "Pertinent Literature" at the end of the guidelines. This could be taken to imply APA recognition of PAS as pertinent to child custody proceedings. Critics may say, "Not so fast, what about the APA's public statement?"

The APA's public stance on PAS is:

> "The American Psychological Association (APA) believes that all mental health practitioners as well as law enforcement officials and the courts must take any reports of domestic violence in divorce and child custody cases seriously. An APA 1996 Presidential Task Force on Violence and the Family noted the lack of data to support so-called "parental alienation syndrome", and raised concern about the term's use. However, we have no official position on the purported syndrome".

It is noteworthy that the APA's Task Force was in 1996, 16 years ago. A lot of work has been done in those years. It is also noteworthy that the APA does not have any public affirmations regarding any other diagnosis. We are not aware of any public statements where the APA publicly declares "clinical depression, schizophrenia, obsessive compulsive disorder, etc... is officially recognized". The American Psychiatric Association publishes the DSM-IV with its "recognized" disorders, not the American Psychological Association. In addition the implication of the APA's statement is that somehow, using the terminology PAS would lead someone to deny or negate the presence of domestic violence. This is clearly not the case and has been discussed beyond sufficiency. And finally, the APA does not have an official position on this disorder or any other one.

Like *Frye and Daubert,* the Federal Rule of Evidence 702 allows the admission of expert scientific opinion only if "scientific, technical, or other specialized knowledge will assist the trier of fact to understand the evidence or to determine a fact in issue..." Under the rule, which has been adopted in identical or substantially similar form by the majority of states, the expert's testimony must be "based on sufficient facts or data," and is "the product of reliable principles and methods." The arguments presented above for PAS meeting the *Frye* and *Daubert* equally apply to the FRE 702. There is sufficient evidence that PAS meets the scientific and technical knowledge to assist courts in understanding the clinical issues in family law cases and especially in child custody cases.

6. PAS is anti-feminist and unfairly blames women

According to Gardner, alienated parents are not guilty of the heinous behaviors that they are accused of which justifies a child's total alienation from them. If, on the other hand, a parent's behavior does justify a child's alienation, this does not quality as PAS. This does not mean that the targeted parent is totally innocent of inappropriate behavior or questionable parenting practices. We must keep in mind that we are working with human beings who are quite fallible. The point, however, is that the child's hatred for the parent is not commensurate with the parent's behavior, with all its imperfections.

When PAS is present and valid the alienating parent and the child are primarily responsible. Similarly, Kelly's (1980) earlier work emphasized the contributions of the aligned parent,

> "The most extreme identification with the parent's cause we have called an 'alignment'- a divorce-specific relationship that occurs when a parent and one or more children join in a vigorous attack on the other parent. It is the embattled parent, often the one who opposes the divorce in the first place, who initiates and fuels the alignment".

Some critics argue that PAS overemphasizes the pathological contributions of the alienating parent while overlooking other possible causes of the child's denigration and rejection of a targeted parent. When critics find fault with Gardner for not recognizing that genuine abuse, neglect, or violent behavior can cause behavior identified as PAS, they clearly have an inadequate understanding of PAS as put forth by Dr. Gardner. It is well recognized that poor parental behavior can cause a child's alienation; but PAS is reserved for alienation that is not warranted by a parent's behavior. Gardner went even further, however he asserted that PAS results from the combination of an alienating parent's influence and the child's own contributions.

Other clinicians believe that Gardner, being psychoanalytically oriented as most psychiatrists, overlooked the importance of family dysfunction in which neither parent can be said to be psychologically healthier than the other. Some assert that PAS is less a psychopathology of one parent but more of a high conflict between both parents, therefore a severe pathology of both parents. Others see PAS as a family dynamic in which all of the family members play a role. Still others feel a particular family dynamic is responsible rather something being induced in the child by an alienating parent.

In working with child custody cases mental health professionals often report clear evidence that an alienating parent is deliberately and knowingly manipulating the child. Even when the manipulation is subtle or operating on an unconscious level, this manipulation and suggestion results because of the power imbalance between parent and child. There is an extensive body of published work that clearly identifies the behavior of alienating parents as abusive. Dr. Warshak (2001) cited numerous works in this paper, there are continual updates to this body of literature. In virtually every study, the inflicting of PAS is commonly documented to be the result of an alienating parent. These studies lend clear support to the position that the core problem in PAS is between the alienating parent and the child.

In some studies other parties, such as relatives and professionals, contribute to the alienation. Some authors have drawn attention to the damage caused by psychotherapists and custody evaluators whose intervention and recommendations reflect an inadequate understanding of PAS. Many professionals accept as valid a child's criticisms of a target parent and thus the professional perpetuates and fosters PAS. In Florida, continuing education for psychologists on assessing sexual abuse cases includes the presumption that abuse allegations by children are usually true and should be readily accepted. Of course this is in total denial of the work by such researchers as Stephen Ceci (1995), author of the book *Jeopardy in the Courtroom*, published by the APA.

7. PAS forces children to be with a "hated" parent who is possibly an abuser

A very controversial issue surrounding PAS is the recommendation of forced visitation and access between a child and the targeted or alienated parent. If the alienation is moderately severe to severe then the access between the child and the alienating parent is recommended to be limited. This makes sense, if the child remains in the toxic influence of a parent the chances of their rehabilitating the other relationship is very unlikely.

Interestingly when the alienation is at a moderate level Gardner recommended a court award primary custody to the alienating parent, appoint a therapist for the family, and enforce the child's contact with the target parent through the threat of imposing sanctions applied to the alienating parent. Such sanctions would be similar to those a court would use with a parent who is in contempt for failure to pay child support. The sanctions could include a continuum from requiring the posting of a bond, fines, community service, probation, house arrest and even short-term incarceration. When courts are reluctant to impose such sanctions, it is all too common that alienating parents have interfered with visitation with the other parent and flaunt court orders with impunity.

In one case we know of, an alienating mother actually placed the children in a psychiatric hospital, multiple times, when it was time for them to visit their father in Florida. The treating psychiatrist knew full well that the children were to visit their father in Florida, but admitted them to the hospital anyway each time. The courts in Florida were helpless to enforce the visitation because the courts in Illinois refused to enforce the visitation. This situation has remedied itself, however, apparently to the satisfaction of the authorities in Illinois. The mother received word from the local Sheriff's office that the following day they were coming to take the children, so the mother kidnapped the children, one of which is severely handicapped and has not been heard from since. An entire book could be written on this one case alone critiquing the condition of the legal, law enforcement and mental health professions regarding this problem.

As Evans (2006) pointed out, the goals of therapy with children diagnosed with PAS are to rehabilitate their relationship with an estranged parent and to foster healthy contact with the alienating parent. Therapeutic interventions should be designed to assist children in developing and maintaining differentiated views of their parents as opposed to polarized views. One way to get children back with the rejected parent is to remove the decision about contact out of their hands and remind them of the impending sanctions against the alienating parent. This gives them an "excuse" to spend time with the target parent; now they would have to visit with them. A therapist working with that child also tries to help them understand that their hatred of the other parent has been influenced by programming. This indoctrination has undermined their ability to reach their own conclusions about their parent which should be based on their own experience with the target. This treatment is similar to the deprogramming techniques that are used with cult victims to counteract the effects of indoctrination.

In some cases, ranging from moderate to severe PAS, where the alienating parent is intensively programming and there is a likely risk that the alienation will become more severe, Gardner recommended a different approach. In such cases he recommended awarding primary custody to the targeted parent and restricting contact between the alienating parent and child. This limited exposure to the alienating parent is done to prevent further indoctrination. If the alienation is severe enough and the alienating parent is likely to persist in their programming then Gardner recommended that the children be removed from the home of the alienating parent. Consider the analogy of working with a child who was kidnapped by a cult. It seems preposterous that we would allow a kidnapped child to maintain in frequent contact with the cult leader while we were rehabilitating their relationship with their biological parents. One reason we would prevent such contact is to eliminate the possibility that they would continue being contaminated. The same applies to an alienating parent. To remain in such a toxic environment would only acerbate the problem.

Sometimes a transitional site is needed in order to rehabilitate the relationship. In severe cases some are so severely alienated that they will not comply with court orders regarding visitation. In addition the alienating parent will not facilitate contact with the target parent and the courts are reluctant to force children to visit with a parent because they express fear of that parent. In such cases they may benefit from a temporary placement in a transitional site before reintegrating the children with the target parent. Possible transitional sites range in restrictiveness from very little to most restrictive, depending on the amount of control needed to ensure the children's cooperation and the alienating parent's compliance with court orders. Such sites can include a grandparent's home or that of a relative or friend. Moving up on the scale of restrictiveness can include a foster home, a community shelter or even a hospital.

Even the threat of a temporary placement in a transitional site may induce a child to cooperate with court-ordered visitation. With an older child (ages 11-16) who refuses visits with the alienated parent, Gardner (2001) suggested finding the child in contempt of court. Gardner has been severely criticized for making this recommendation, not only has this met with severe opposition, but he has been routinely misquoted about this issue.

Gardner had warned against unnecessary indulging of children's visitation refusal. He believed the best way to reverse alienation is to provide a child with direct experiences which can counteract negative programming and correct the child's distorted perceptions of the targeted parent. Supervised visitation, on the other hand, sends the message that the child's fears of the targeted parent are rational and that the court agrees that the child needs some sort of protection from the alienated parent. Rather than increase the child's sense of security around the targeted parent, it may reinforce the child's uneasiness.

The results reported in *Children Held Hostage* (Clawar & Rivlin, 1991), the ABA sponsored study, supported a firmer approach to enforcing parent-child contact.

> "One of the most powerful tools the courts have is the threat and implementation of environmental modification. Of the approximately four hundred cases we have seen where the courts have increased the contact with the target parent (and in half of these, over the objection of the children), there has been positive change in 90 percent of the relationships between the child and the target parent, including the elimination or reduction of many social-psychological, educational, and physical problems that the child presented prior to the modification".

Gardner conducted and reported a follow-up study of 99 children diagnosed with PAS and he found a strong correlation between environmental modification and reduction in PAS symptoms. In 22 instances, the alienated child's contact with the rejected parent was increased and contact with the alienating parent was decreased. In all 22 cases, PAS symptoms were reduced or eliminated. By contrast, only 9% of the children (7 out of 77) whose contact with the rejected parent was not increased by the court, showed a reduction in PAS symptoms.

Ten years after Dr. Warshak (2001) wrote his article it continues to be the case that all the published findings on treatment outcomes support the effectiveness of enforcing contact between the child and alienated parent and no findings oppose this policy. When a robust body of literature available point to the same conclusion, we need to pay attention while allowing for the possibility that the circumstances of any single case may dictate an alternative treatment approach.

No consensus, however, exists to recommend to the courts to transfer custody (as opposed to enforced contact) in severe PAS cases. There has been expressed concern that alienated children cannot cope with the change in custody and they could be seriously harmed. While it is certainly a possibility however, if this result were likely, it would not be unreasonable to find such reporting in the professional literature. There is no published documentation of such harm. Some clinicians actually advise parents of severely alienated children to accept the loss of their children and simply hope for a possible future reconciliation. This flies in the face of Clawar's and Rivlin's (1991) conclusion:

> "Caution must be exercised in judging that the point of no return has been reached. We have seen numerous cases where children have been successfully deprogrammed by making radical changes in their living arrangements—often with appropriate legal interventions".

They explain:

"There are risks incumbent in any process; however, *a decision has to be made as to what is the greater risk*. It is usually more damaging socially, psychologically, educationally, and/or physically for children to maintain beliefs, values, thoughts, and behaviors that disconnect them from one of their parents (or from telling the truth, as in a criminal case) compared to getting rid of the distortions or false statements".

One of the most recent advances in correcting the PAS situation is an effort developed and spearheaded by no other than Dr. Richard A. Warshak. Dr. Warshak, by the way, is the author of *Divorce Poison* (2001) an excellent resource on alienation. His program, *Family Bridges: a Workshop for Troubled and Alienated Parent-Child Relationships* is an innovative educational and experiential program that helps severely and unreasonably alienated children and adolescents adjust to living with a parent they claim to hate or fear. According to Warshak's website, Family Bridges offers a safe and secure environment that gives participants, in four consecutive days, what they need to restore a normal relationship. Beyond reconnecting children with their parents, Family Bridges teach children how to think critically and how to maintain balanced, realistic, and compassionate views of both parents. They also help them develop skills to resist outside pressures that can lead them to act against their judgment-a valuable lesson for teens. Warshak teaches parents how to sensitively manage their children's behavior, and gives the family tools to effectively communicate and manage conflicts. The children and the rejected parent go through Family Bridges together as one family, and not with a group of families. This allows them to tailor the program to meet the exact needs of each individual family. Usually Family Bridges takes place in a vacation setting, although in some cases we conduct the program in the family home.

The research on the effectiveness of this program is extremely encouraging. It is highly likely that we will be hearing a lot more about this extremely promising program.

8. PAS is not in the DSM-IV therefore it doesn't exist

We have saved the least of the eight controversies for the last. Having said that, there are other issues surrounding PAS but it is not the intent of this work to be exhaustive of all of them.   This one, however, is interesting because it is frequently raised by professionals who really should know better.

There are some who claim that there is no such thing as PAS. The argument given to justify this assertion is that PAS does not in appear in DSM-IV. To say that PAS does not exist because it is not listed in DSM-IV clearly indicates ignorance about the DSM or its history.   In 1980, Auto- immune Deficiency Syndrome (AIDS) did not exist because it was not then listed in medical textbooks.

The DSM uses committees to meet, present and review pertinent literature regarding diagnostic entities. Sometimes this process takes a considerable length of time, many years. For example, Gille de La Tourette first described his syndrome, later to become a disorder, in 1885. It was not until 95 years later, that the disorder was finally listed in the DSM. Another example was Asperger who first described his syndrome in 1957. In 1994, 37 years later, it was accepted into DSM-IV.   Like Tourettes, Asperger's *Syndrome* also became Asperger's *Disorder*. While these may seem a little odd because of the rarity of the disorders, a more recent example is PTSD, reference to this was made earlier. PTSD "did not exist" until relatively recently.

If you think it took a long time for Tourettes to get into the DSM, consider PTSD. It was first described in 1900 BC by an Egyptian physician who stated it was a "hysterical" reaction to trauma. Now, was this guy a little ahead of the curve or what? Later it was described as "railway spine", a nineteenth-century diagnosis for PTSD symptoms of survivors of railroad accidents. Its description was published in 1864. They thought the symptoms were due to the excessive speeds of trains in their day which was about 30 miles an hour and the human body could not deal with such speeds. The military, since the Civil War, have recorded PTSD symptoms of veterans who suffered emotional problems and were diagnosed with "soldier's heart". The term "shell shock" came into existence during World War I and then in WWII it became "combat fatigue, war neurosis and operational exhaustion". It was not until 1980 that PTSD made its way into the DSM-III. It was said that the development of PTSD, in part, had a socio-economic and political implication. While the military for a long time recognized this disorder the victims did not receive economic compensation because there was no psychiatric diagnosis; it didn't exist. It was not until after the Vietnam War did this situation change. So the argument that PAS does not exist because it is not in the DSM is not very persuasive.

PAS was first publicized in 1985 and the current edition of the DSM-IV was published in 1994. There was only six years from its inception to the time the DSM committees were meeting from 1991 to 1993. There simply was not enough published research on PAS for the committees to consider even if it was submitted for consideration. This, of course, is no longer the case. To say that the DSM includes only those disorders that have been subjected to extensive research and peer review is a little misleading. Yes the process is pedantic but it is not infallible.

In 2008 William Bernet, M.D. took up the daunting task of pulling together professionals from all over the world to support an effort of proposing a new diagnosis of Parent

Alienation Disorder to the DSM-5 Task Force of the American Psychiatric Association. The decision making process continues to this date, so we cannot end this work with a definitive statement relative to the office status of the new disorder; that will have to wait for another day. But it is noteworthy to observe that PAS has been recognized in 30 countries around the world involving too many professionals to give an accurate count.

Epilogue

Despite an ever growing literature, the diagnosis of Parental Alienation Syndrome (PAS) continues to stir controversy in both the legal and mental health professions. We tried to provide a relatively brief overview of PAS, the symptoms, the various manifestations, some strategies of working with inflicted families and we addressed the major controversies.

PAS is very real; it is very valid; and it is very well documented. The phenomenon admittedly needs more research and discussion; there is no doubt about it. Our focus should, however, be on the harm PAS does to children, especially when they lose their relationship with a loving parent. In fact when PAS is not acknowledged it can be life-threatening. Pamela Richardson (2006), mother and author of the book *A Kidnapped Mind,* describes the torment PAS caused her son, who tragically, at age 16, committed suicide.

Indeed, domestic violence and child abuse need to be eradicated. But PAS is nothing short of severe emotional and mental child abuse. To deny its existence is, in itself, abusive. The act of interfering in a child's relationship with a loving parent not only causes a great deal of pain to the target parent but, can bring a life-long experience of pain and destruction to the child. Parents, who would substitute the needs of their child with their own self-centered and self-gratifying needs, are abusive parents. It is these parents who will misuse the argument of PAS against the other parent. The fact that a true abuser will use the diagnosis to their advantage in order to hurt another parent is not a strike against the diagnosis of PAS, but it is a strike against those agencies and individuals that fall victim to the lies of an abusive parent. The best protection against these lies is knowledge, education and training.

The best way to counter the misunderstanding by courts is not to deny the existence of PAS, but to work toward awareness and education. In that way, soon, the courts will understand that not only is PAS afoot, but they will know who the true perpetrators of alienation are.

We truly hope this work is a contribution to your clinical practice, if you are in a profession in the family law arena, and to your life, if you are a parent. We are grateful and honored that you chose to read this book.

The Authors

Appendix A

Directions for the PA/PAS Journal

This is a tool to be used to document situations and incidents that may be related to PA/PAS in a case. The journal can be completed by either litigants or professionals wishing to keep track of incidents either as they occur or as a summary while reviewing case facts. As evidence regarding each of the symptoms surfaces, the Journal keeper should document the specific evidence related to the symptoms so they will have a handy summary reference of the symptoms, details of related incidents and if applicable the source of the description. Be as specific as you can and include dates and documents that provide information on each symptom.

PA Criteria
Access or visitation blocking by one parent
This criterion refers to the phenomenon of one parent attempting, and at times succeeding, at preventing a child from being with the other parent.

False allegations of abuse
The alienating parent must provide reasons as to why the child should not see that other parent. Invariably, the reasons given are that the other parent is in some way abusive, neglectful and incompetent; therefore they pose a danger to the child.

Deterioration in the relationship between the children and the Target Parent
This criterion refers to the effects of the first two. The relationship with a parent deteriorates. This occurs on two levels: externally and internally.

> **External deterioration** refers to how a child behaves in the company of various audiences.
> **Internal deterioration** refers to the actual subjective deterioration of the child's view of the other parent.

Fear reaction regarding displeasing the Alienating Parent.

These children have been taught that they have already been abandoned by one parent, fear of further abandonment runs very deeply. It is important, therefore, to understand that the fear is actually a fear of loss of that remaining parent. It is this fear that fuels and drives the internal changes that occur in alienated children.

PAS Symptoms

The campaign of denigration

This refers to a child's view of the "hated" or targeted parent. First, the campaign of denigration refers to the one being waged by the accusing or alienating parent in his or her indoctrination of the child. The other component is the child's own contribution in this denigration process. This second component is critical. Without it, the child is not truly alienated. With it, however, the alienating parent can "sit back" and let the child be the voice of criticism of the Target Parent.

Weak or frivolous rationalizations for the deprecation

This typically refers to a child not wanting to suddenly be with a parent for reasons that do not warrant such a position.

Lack of ambivalence

This criterion refers to the alienated child's "all good" portrayal of the Alienating Parent and "all bad" portrayal of the Targeted Parent.

The "Independent Thinker" phenomenon

Here the child maintains that his or her criticisms of the Targeted Parent are the result of his or her own independent thought and not the product of coaching by anyone especially the Alienating Parent.

Reflexive support of the Alienating Parent in the parental conflict

This symptom refers to the child's consistent loyalty to the alienating parent's position, never defending or siding with the targeted parent.

Absence of guilt over cruelty to and/or exploitation of the Target Parent

It represents a diminishing and ultimately extinction of the child's ability to empathize and not just with the targeted parent. It is tied to conscience and moral choice and may set a lifelong pattern of reacting to stress and threatening situations.

Presence of borrowed scenarios

This symptom refers to the making up of stories and incidents in the furtherance of the vilification of the Target Parent. The quality of the stories and the details of the incidents often reflect that of the alienating parent, hence the "borrowed" nature of the scenarios.

Spread of animosity to the extended family of the Target Parent

This refers to a child being alienated not only from the Target Parent, but from the Target Parent's entire life, his or her activities, and his or her loved ones, such as grandparents, aunts, uncles, etc. As with the targeted parent, these children had a history of having a loving and caring relationship with the extended family members.

PA/PAS Journal[©]

Date:_____ **Time:**_____
Location: _____
Parties Present: _____

SITUATION	PA/PAS
	Visitation Blocking
	False Allegations of Abuse
	Deterioration in Relationship
	Exaggerated Fear of Alienating Parent
	Campaign of Denigration
	Weak, Frivolous, Absurd Reasons
	Lack of Ambivalence
	Independent Thinker
	Reflexive Support
	Absence of Guilt
	Borrowed Scenarios
	Spread of Animosity

YOUR REACTION / RESPONSE	THEIR REACTION

References

American Psychiatric Association, *Diagnostic and Statistical Manual of Mental Disorders, Third Edition-Revised* Washington, DC, American Psychiatric Association, 1987.

American Psychological Association: Guidelines for child custody evaluations in divorce proceedings. *American Psychologist* 1994; 49:7:677-680.

Baker, A.: *Adult Children of Parental Alienation Syndrome* New York, NY, W. W. Norton & Co. 2007.

Bernet, W., Eds.: *Parental Alienation, DSM=5, and ICD-11.* Springfield, IL, Charles C. Thomas, 2010.

Blush, G. J., Ross, K. L.: Sexual abuse validity discriminators in the divorced or divorcing family *Issues in Child Abuse Accusations* 1990; 2:1-6.

Blush, G. J., Ross, K. L.: investigation and case management issues and strategies *Issues in Child Abuse Accusations* 1990; 2:152-160.

Bone, J. M., Walsh, M. R.: Parental alienation syndrome: how to detect it and what to do about it *The Florida Bar J* 1999; 73:44-48.

Burrill, J., *Parent alienation syndrome in court referred custody cases* Dissertation North Central University Prescott Valley, Arizona (2001).

Ceci, S. J., Bruck, M.: *Jeopardy in the Courtroom: A Scientific Analysis of Children's Testimony* Washington, DC, American Psychological Association, 1995.

Clawar, S. S., Rivlin, B.V.: *Children Held Hostage: Dealing with Programmed and Brainwashed Children* Chicago, American Bar Association, 1991.

Daubert v Merrell Dow Pharmaceuticals, Inc., 509 U.S. 579 (1993).

Diagnostic and Statistical Manual of Mental Disorders, Fourth Edition Washington, DC, American Psychiatric Association, 1994.

Evans, R. A.: Treatment Considerations with Children Diagnosed with PAS. *The Florida Bar J* 2006; 80:4; 69-72.

Robert Franklin, Unpublished summary of the" Long term History of PAS", 2009

Frye v United States 293 F. 1013 (1923).

Gardner, R. A.: *Therapeutic Interventions for Children with Parental Alienation Syndrome* Cresskill, NJ, Creative Therapeutics, 2001.

Gardner, R. A.: *Addendum to The Parental Alienation Syndrome: A Guide for Mental Health and Legal Professionals (2nd edition)* Cresskill, NJ, Creative Therapeutics, 2000. www.rgardner.com/refs/addendum2.html.

Gardner, R. A.: *The Parental Alienation Syndrome: A Guide for Mental Health and Legal Professionals (2nd edition)* Cresskill, NJ, Creative Therapeutics, 1998.

Gardner, R. A.: Recent trends in divorce and custody litigation. *Academy Forum* 1985:2:3-7.

Gardner, R. A., Sauber, S. R. & Demosthenes, L. (Eds.) *The international handbook of parental alienation syndrome: Conceptual, clinical and legal considerations* Springfield, Illinois: Charles C. Thomas, 2006.

Hendricks, H.: *Getting The Love You Want: A Guide For Couples* New York, Holt, 1988.

Jacobs, J. W.: Euripides' Medea: A psychodynamic model of severe divorce pathology. *American Journal of Psychotherapy,* 1988; XLII: 2:308-319.

Johnston J. R, Campbell, LE: *Impasses of Divorce: The Dynamics and Resolution of Family Conflict*. New York, Free Press, 1988.

Kelly, J. B., Johnston JR: The alienated child: a reformulation of parental alienation syndrome *Family Ct Rev*(2001); 39(3):249-66.

Kilgore v. Boyd, 13th Circuit Court, Hillsborough County, No. 94-7573 (Fla. Nov. 22, 2000).

Rand, D. C.: The spectrum of parental alienation syndrome (part I) *Am J Forensic Psychology* 1997; 15:3:23-51.

Reich, W.: *Character Analysis* New York, Farrar, Straus and Giroux, 1949.

Richardson, P. (2006) A kidnapped mind: A mother's heartbreaking memoir of parental alienation Toronto: Dundurm.

Turkat, I. D.: Child visitation interference in divorce *Clinical Psychology Review* 1994; 14:732 742.

Wallerstein, J. S., Blakeslee, S.: *Second Chances: Men, Women, and Children a Decade After Divorce* New York, Ticknor and Fields, 1989.

Wallerstein, J. S., Kelly, J. B.: *Surviving the Breakup* New York, Basic Books, 1980.

Warshak R. A.: *Divorce Poison: Protecting the Parent-Child Bond from a Vindictive Ex* New York, Regan Books, 2001.

Warshak, R. A.: Current controversies regarding parental alienation syndrome *American Journal of Forensic Psychology,* 2001; 19:3:29-59.

Made in United States
Troutdale, OR
08/07/2023